William Ewart Gladstone

Impregnable Rock of Holy Scripture

William Ewart Gladstone

Impregnable Rock of Holy Scripture

ISBN/EAN: 9783337289843

Printed in Europe, USA, Canada, Australia, Japan

Cover: Foto ©Lupo / pixelio.de

More available books at **www.hansebooks.com**

THE
IMPREGNABLE ROCK
OF
HOLY SCRIPTURE.

HENRY ALTEMVS

THE IMPREGNABLE ROCK OF HOLY SCRIPTURE

GLADSTONE

PHILADELPHIA

WILLIAM EWART GLADSTONE

WILLIAM E. GLADSTONE

THE
IMPREGNABLE
ROCK OF
HOLY SCRIPTURE

PHILADELPHIA
HENRY ALTEMUS

PREFATORY NOTE.

THE additions, which in the course of revision have been made to these Essays, are in the nature of amplified or newly supplied argument, and do not affect their general tenor.

In the *Jewish Chronicle* of September 12, 1890, I find a paragraph which appears to approve the general argument of my article on "The Mosaic Legislation," but impugns the statement that the Massorites were a body without a parallel in history, and that the Hebrews were alone in building up a regularly scientific method of handling the material forms of their sacred oracles. I have not the slightest pretension to speak with authority upon this subject, and I did no more than endeavor to report faithfully what I gathered from trustworthy sources. But I have no reason to believe that my readers have been misled. As regards the Hindus, I understand it is stated that they counted verses, words, syllables, and letters; but it does not appear that this statement is one historically authenticated. Even if it were so, and if we add that the Samaritans imitated the proceedings of their Jewish brethren, and that similar enumeration was made by Syrians or others, yet the answer remains that such a computation is a very small component part of the Massorah, and can no more be called an equivalent to it than a human limb can be called a human body. To the Massorah, so far as I can learn, there is nothing approaching an equivalent. As respects the Greeks, they had no sacred writings at all; and I am unaware of their having used, in any case, any such method as is here in question.

CONTENTS.

		PAGE
I.	FIRST VIEW OF THE IMPREGNABLE ROCK OF HOLY SCRIPTURE	9
II.	THE CREATION STORY	39
III.	THE OFFICE AND WORK OF THE OLD TESTAMENT IN OUTLINE	95
IV.	THE PSALMS	141
V.	THE MOSAIC LEGISLATION	189
VI.	ON THE RECENT CORROBORATIONS OF SCRIPTURE FROM THE REGIONS OF HISTORY AND NATURAL SCIENCE	239
VII.	CONCLUSION	279

First View of the Impregnable Rock of Holy Scripture.

First View of the Impregnable Rock of Holy Scripture.

IT is a serious question how far one ignorant, like myself, of Hebrew, and having no regular practice in the study and explanation of the text of the Old Testament, is entitled to attempt representations concerning it, which must present more or less the character of advice, to any portion of his fellow-countrymen. It is clear that he can draw no sufficient warrant for such a course from the mere warmth of his desire to arrest a prevailing mischief, or from his fear lest any portion of the public should lose or relax unawares their hold upon the Book which Christendom regards as an inestimable treasure, and thereby bring upon themselves, as well as others, an inexpressible calamity. But, on the other hand, he has some better pleas to urge. The first is, that there is a very large section of the community whose opportunities or judgment have been materially smaller than his own. The second is, that though he is greatly wanting in the valuable qualifications which grow out of special study in this field, he has, for more than forty years (believing that change of labor is to a great extent the healthiest form of recreation), devoted the larger part of all such time as he could properly withdraw from political duties to another, and in several respects a similar, field of specialism; namely, the earnest study of prehistoric antiquity and of its documents in regard to the Greek race, whose destinies have been, after those of the Hebrews, the most wonderful in themselves, and the most fertile of results for us, among all the races of mankind. As between this field, which has for its central point the study of Homer, and that of the early Scriptures, which may in the mass be roughly called contemporary with the Homeric period, much light is, and with the progress of research more can hardly fail to be, given and received. Moreover, I have there had the opportunity of perceiving how, among specialists as with other men, there may be fashions of the time and school, which Lord Bacon called idols of the market-place, and currents of prejudice below the surface, such as to detract somewhat from the authority which each inquirer might justly claim in his own field, and from their title to impose their conclusions upon mankind. As a judicious artist likes to know the opinion even of one not an expert on his picture, and sometimes derives benefit from it, so in all studies lights may be thrown inwards from without; and this in far the largest degree where the special branch deals with a subject-matter that both takes deep root in our nature, and is the source of profoundly interesting controversies for mankind at large. Yet I do not feel sure that these considerations would have led me to make the present attempt, were they not capped with another of great importance. It appears to me that we may grant, for argument's sake, to the negative or destructive specialist in the field of the ancient Scriptures all which as a specialist he can by possibility be entitled to ask, respecting the age, text, and authorship of the books, and yet may hold firmly, as firmly as of old, to the ideas justly conveyed by the title I have adopted for these papers, and may invite our fellow-men to stand along with us on "the impregnable rock of Holy Scripture."

These words sound like a challenge. And they are a challenge to some extent, but not in the sense that might be supposed. They are a challenge to accept the Scriptures on the moral and spiritual and historical ground of their character in themselves, and of the work which they, and the agencies associated with them, have done in the world for some thousands of years, and are doing still. We may, without touching the domain of the critic, contend for them as corresponding by their contents to the idea of a Divine revelation to man. We are entitled to attempt to show that they afford that kind of proof of such a revelation, which is analogous to the known divine operations in other spheres; which binds us as to conduct; and which in other matters, from the simple fact that we are rational beings, we recognize as entitled so to bind us. And again, we may legitimately ask whether they do not differ in such a manner from the other documents of historic and prehistoric religions, while these too are precious in various ways, as to make them witnesses and buttresses to the office of Holy Scripture, rather than sharers in it, although in their degree they may be this also.

But all these assertions lie within the moral and spiritual precinct. No one of them begs any literary question of Old Testament criticism. They leave absolutely open every issue that has been or can be raised respecting the origin, date, authorship and text of the sacred books, which for the present purpose we do not require even to call sacred. Indeed it may be that this destructive criticism, if entirely made good, would, in the view of an inquiry really searching, comprehensive, and philosophical, leave as its result not less but greater reason for admiring the hidden modes by which the great Artificer works out His designs. For, in proportion as the means are feeble, perplexed, and to all appearance confused, is the marvel of the results that are made to stand before our eyes. And the upshot may come to be, that, on this very ground we may have to cry out with the Psalmist* absorbed in worshipping admiration, " Oh, that men would therefore praise the Lord for His goodness, and declare the wonders that He doeth for the children of men ! " For " How unsearchable are His judgments, and His ways past finding out." For the memories of men, and the art of writing, and the care of the copyist, and the tablet and the rolls of parchment, are but the secondary or mechanical means by which the Word has been carried down to us along the river of the ages ; and the natural and inherent weakness of these means is but a special tribute to the grandeur and vastness of the end, and of Him that wrought it out.

So, then, these high-sounding words have been placed in the foreground of the present

* Ps. cvii. 8.

observations, because they convey in a positive and definite manner the conclusion which the observations themselves aim at sustaining, at least in outline, on general grounds of reason, and at enforcing as a commanding rule of thought and life. They lead upwards and onwards to the idea that the Scriptures are well called Holy Scriptures; and that, though assailed by camp, by battery, and by mine, they are nevertheless a house builded upon a rock, and that rock impregnable; that the weapon of offence, which shall impair their efficiency for aiding in the redemption of mankind, has not yet been forged; that the Sacred Canon, which it took (perhaps) two thousand years from the accumulations of Moses down to the acceptance of the Apocalypse to construct, is like to wear out the storms and the sunshine of the world, and all the wayward aberrations of humanity, not merely for a term as long, but until time shall be no more.

And yet, upon the very threshold, I embrace, in what I think a substantial sense, one of the great canons of modern criticism, which teaches us that the Scriptures are to be treated like any other book in the trial of their title. The volume, which is put into our hands when young under that venerated name, is, like any other volume, made with paper, types and ink, and has been put together as a material object by human hands. The many and diversified utterances it contains proceeded from the mouth or pen of men; and the question, whether and in what degree, through supernatural guidance, they were, for this purpose, more than men, is to be determined, like other disputable questions, by the evidence. The books have been transmitted to us from their formation onwards in perishable materials, and from remote dates. They were so transmitted, until four hundred years ago, by the agency of copyists, as in the case of other literary productions, and presumably with a like liability to casual error or to fraudulent handling. That in some sense the Holy Scriptures contain something of a human element is clear, as to the New Testament, from diversities of reading, from slight conflicts in the narrative, and from an insignificant number of controverted cases as to the authenticity of the text. We have also the Latin Vulgate partially competing with the Greek original, on the ground that it has been more or less founded on manuscripts older than any we now possess. As regards the Old Testament, we find the established Hebrew Text to be founded on MSS. of a date not earlier than (I believe) the tenth century of our era. It is, moreover, at variance in many points with the Greek version, commonly termed the Septuagint; which is considered to date wholly or in the main from the third century before the Advent of our Saviour, and the framers of which had before them copies older by more than a thousand years. Thus the accuracy of the text, the age and authorship of the books, open up a vast field of purely literary controversy; and such a question as whether the closing verses of St. Mark's Gospel* have the authority of Scripture must be determined by literary evidence, as much as the genuineness of the pretended preface to the Æneid, or of a particular stanza which appears in an ode of Catullus.†

Towards summing up these observations, I will remind the reader that those who believe in a Divine Revelation, as pervading or as contained in the Scriptures, and especially those who accept the full doctrine of literalism as to the vehicle of that inspiration, have to lay their account with the following (among other) considerations, which it is hard for them to repudiate as

---

* I have never seen a confutation of the reasonings of Dean Burgon in his treatise on this subject. He supports the text as it stands. The marginal note in the Revised Version is surely unsatisfactory, for it does not tell the whole case, but only a part, about the manuscripts.

† Carm. LII. 13-16.

inadmissible. There may possibly have been—

1. Imperfect comprehension of that which was divinely communicated :
2. Imperfect expression of what had once been comprehended :
3. Lapse of memory in oral transmission :
4. Errors of copyists in written transmission :
5. Changes with the lapse of time in the sense of words :
6. Variations arising from renderings into different tongues, especially as between the Hebrew text and the Septuagint :
7. The inspired writers of the New Testament varied in the text they used for citations from the Old Testament, and did not regard either the Hebrew or the Greek as of exclusive authority :
8. There are three variant chronologies of the Old Testament, according to the Hebrew, the Septuagint, and the Samaritan Pentateuch respectively; and it would be unwarrantable to claim for any one of them, as against the others, the absolute sanction of a Divine revelation : while an historical argument of some importance may be deducible, on the other hand, from the fact that their variations lie within certain limits.

No doubt there will be those who will resent any association between the idea of a

Divine revelation and the possibility of even the smallest intrusion of error into its vehicle. This idea, however, is by no means altogether a novelty. It is manifestly included as a likelihood, if not a certainty, in the fact of continuous transmission by human means, without continuous miracle to guarantee it. But further, ought they not to bear in mind that we are bound by the rule of reason to look for the same method of procedure in this great matter of a written provision of Divine knowledge for our needs, as in the other parts of the manifold dispensation under which Providence has placed us. Now that method or principle is one of sufficiency, not of perfection; of sufficiency for the attainment of practical ends, not of conformity to ideal standards; and the question what constitutes that sufficiency is a matter no more to be judged of by us in relation to the Scriptures, than in relation to any other part of the Divine dispensations, on all of which the Almighty appears to have reserved His judgment to Himself. Bishop Butler, I think, would wisely tell us that we are not the judges, and that we are quite unfit to be the judges, what may be the proper amount and the just conditions of any of the aids to be afforded us in passing through the discipline of life. I will only remark that this default of ideal perfection, this use of twilight instead of a noonday blaze, may be adapted to our weakness, and may be among the appointed means of exercising, and by exercise of strengthening our faith. But what properly belongs to the present occasion is to point out that if probability, and not demonstration, marks the Divine guidance of our paths in life as a whole, we are not entitled to require that when the Almighty, in His mercy, makes a special addition by revelation to what He has already given to us of knowledge in Nature and in Providence, that special gift should be unlike His other gifts, and should have all its lines and limits drawn out with mathematical precision.

I have then admitted, I hope in terms of sufficient fulness, that my aim in no way embraces a controversy with the moderate, or even with the extreme, developments of textual criticism. Dr. Driver, the Regius Professor of Hebrew at Oxford,* personally as well as officially a champion of the doctrine that there is a Divine revelation, has recently shown with great clearness and ability that the basis of such criticism is sound and undeniable, whatever be its liability to aberration either in method or in details. It compares consistencies and inconsistencies of text, not simply as would

* *Contemporary Review*, February, 1890, pp. 215–231.

be done by an ordinary reader, but with all the lights of collateral knowledge. It pronounces on the meaning of terms with the authority derived from thorough acquaintance with a given tongue, or with language at large. It investigates and applies those laws of growth, which operate upon language as they operate in regard to a physical organism.

It has long been known, for example, that portions of the historical books of the Old Testament, such as the Books of Chronicles, were of a date very far later than most of the events which they record, and it is widely believed* that a portion of the prophecies included in the Book of Isaiah were later than his time. It is now pressed upon us that, according to the prevailing judgment of the learned, the form in which the older books of the Old Testament have come down to us does not correspond as a rule with their titles, and is due to later though still, as is largely held, to remote periods; and that the law presented to us in the Pentateuch is not an enactment of a single date, but has been enlarged by a process of growth, and by gradual accretions. To us

---

* I am not aware, however, what is the reply to the arguments of Mr. Urwick, who contends for the unity of authorship. ("The Servant of Jehovah." Edinburgh: Clark. 1877.)

who are without original means of judgment these are, at first hearing, without doubt, disturbing announcements. Yet common sense requires us to say, let them be fought out by the competent, but let not us who are incompetent interfere. I utterly, then, eschew for myself the responsibility of conflict with these properly critical conclusions.

But this acquiescence is subject to the following remarks. First, the acceptance of the conclusions of the critics has reference to the present literary form of the works, and leaves entirely open every question relating to the substance. Any one who reads the books of the Pentateuch, from the second to the fifth, must observe how little they present the appearance of consecutive, coherent, and digested record. But their several portions must be considered on the evidence applicable to them respectively. And the main facts of the history they contain have received strong confirmation from Egyptian and Eastern research. With regard to the Book of Genesis, the admission which has been made implies nothing adverse to the truth of the traditions it embodies, nothing adverse to their antiquity, nothing which excludes or discredits, as to the older among them, the idea of their having originally formed part of a primitive revelation, simultaneous or successive. The forms of expression may have changed, yet the substance may remain with an altered literary form; as some scholars have thought (not, I believe, rightly) that the diction and modelling of the Homeric Poems is comparatively modern, and yet the matter they embody may belong to a remote antiquity. It is also conceivable that the diction of Chaucer, for example, might be altered so as to conform to the usage of the nineteenth century, and to leave little apparent resemblance to the original, and yet the whole substance of Chaucer might remain.

Further, our assent to the conclusions of the critics ought to be strictly limited to a provisional and revocable assent; and this on practical grounds of stringent obligation. For, firstly, these conclusions appear to be in a great measure floating and uncertain, to be the subject of manifold controversy. Secondly, they seem to shift and vary with rapidity in the minds of those who hold them. In editing and revising the work of Bleek,* Wellhausen accepts in a great degree

* "Einleitung in das Alte Testament," Haupttheil I., C. Die Psalmen. [The edition published and adopted by Wellhausen, to which I refer, is dated 1878; but the book had been published in 1860.] So recently as in the fifth edition (Berlin, 1886), the Bleek-Wellhausen work assigns much weight to the Davidic titles; gives to David nearly fifty Psalms; and holds that there is no Psalm later than Nehemiah, few so late. (Sections 220-22, pages, 457–464, of the *Einleitung*.)

the genuineness of those Davidic Psalms which are contained in the First Book of the Psalter. But I have been told that this position has been abandoned, and that, standing as he appears to do at the head of the negative critics, he now brings down the general body of the Psalms to a date very greatly below that of the Babylonic exile. It is certainly unreasonable to hold a critic to his conclusions without exception. But, on the other hand, it may be asked whether, in order to warrant confidence, they ought not to exhibit some element of stability? The opening of new sources of information may justify all changes fairly referable to them; and in minor matters the finer touches of the destructive, as well as the constructive, artist may be needed to complete his work. But if reasonable grounds for change do not determine its bounds, there must be limits on the other hand to the duty of deference and submission on the part of the outer and uninstructed world, with respect to these literary conclusions. It seems doubtful how far they present to us that aggregate continuity and progression, which the whole world recognizes in the case of the physical sciences; and the most liberal estimate can hardly carry them farther than this, that we should keep an open mind till the cycle of change has been run through, and till time has been given for the detection of flaws, and for the hearing of those whose researches may have led them to different results.

In the present instance we have an example, which may not be without force, in support of this warning. Mr. Margoliouth, the Laudian Professor of Arabic at Oxford, and a gentleman of early academical distinctions altogether extraordinary, has published his Inaugural Lecture,* in which he states his belief that, from materials and by means which he lucidly explains, it will be found possible to reconstruct the Semitic original, hitherto unknown, of the Book of Ecclesiasticus. It was written, as he states, by Ben Sira, not in the Hebrew of the Prophets, but in the later Hebrew of the Rabbis (p. 6). I understand that there are three great stages, or states, of the Hebrew tongue: the Ancient, the Middle, and the New; and that of these the earlier or classical Scriptures belong to the first, and the Book of Nehemiah (for example) to the second. The third is the Rabbinical stage. The passage from one to another of these stages is held, under the laws which determine the movement of that language, to require a very long time. Professor Margoliouth finds

* "On the place of Ecclesiasticus in Semitic Literature." Clarendon Press, 1890.

that Ben Sira wrote in Rabbinical Hebrew, and the earlier we find Rabbinical Hebrew in use, the farther we drive into antiquity the dates of books written in middle and in ancient Hebrew. Suppose, by way of illustration, that Professor Margoliouth shows Rabbinical Hebrew to have come into use two hundred years earlier than had been supposed, the effect is to throw back by two hundred years the latest date to which a book in middle or in ancient Hebrew could be assigned. No wonder, then, that Professor Margoliouth observes (p. 22)—

"Some students are engaged in bringing down the date of every chapter in the Bible so late as to leave no room for prophecy and revelation."

But he goes on to add that if, by the task which he has undertaken, and by those who may follow and improve upon him, this Book shall be properly restored,

"Others will endeavor to find out how early the professedly post-exilian books can be put back, so as to account for the divergence between their awkward Middle-Hebrew and the rich and eloquent New-Hebrew of Ben Sira. However this may be, hypotheses, which place any portion of the classical or Old-Hebrew Scriptures between the Middle-Hebrew of Nehemiah and the New-Hebrew of Ben Sira, will surely require some reconsideration, or at least have to be harmonized in some way with the history of the language, before they can be unconditionally accepted."

Hence the spectator from without, perceiving that there is war, waged on critical grounds, in the critical camp itself, may surmise that what has been wittily called the order of disorder is more or less menaced in its central seat; and he may be the more hardened in his determination not to rush prematurely to final conclusions on the serious, though not as I suppose vital, question respecting the age and authenticity of the early books of the Old Testament in their present literary form.

There is such a thing as mistaking the indifferent for the essential, and as a slavish adherence to traditions insufficiently examined. But the liabilities of human nature to error do not all lie on one side. It may on the contrary be stated with some confidence that, when error in a certain direction after a long precedence is effectively called to account, it is generally apt, and in some cases certain, to be followed by a reign of prejudices, or biassed judgments, more or less extended, and in a contrary direction. There is such a thing as a warping of the mind in favor of disintegration. Often does a critic bring to the book he examines the conclusion which he believes that he has drawn from it. Often when he has not thus imported it, yet the first view, in remote perspective, of the proposition to which he leans will induce him to rush at the most formidable fences that lie straight ahead of him, instead of taking his chances of arriving at it by the common road of reason. And often, even when he has attained his conclusion without prejudice, he will after adopting defend it against objectors, not with argument only, but with all the pride and pain of wounded self-love. And every one of these dangers is commonly enhanced in something like the same proportion, in which the particular subject-matter embraces the highest interests of mankind.

What I would specially press upon those to whom I write is, that they should look broadly and largely at the subject of Holy Scripture, especially of the Scriptures of the older dispensation, which are, so to speak, farther from the eye, and should never allow themselves to be won away from that broad and large contemplation into discussions which, though in their own place legitimate, nay, needful, yet are secondary, and therefore, when substituted for the primary, are worse than frivolous. I do not ask this from them as philosophers or as Christians, but as men of sense. I ask them to look at the subject as they would look at the British Constitution, or at the poetry of Shakespeare. If we were pressed by the apparent absurdity that any one branch of the British Legislature can stop the proceedings of the whole, or that the House of Commons can reduce to beggary the whole Army, Navy, and Civil Service of the country, and that neither law nor usage makes any provision for meeting the case, and this although there would ensue from it nothing less than a frustration of the purposes for which men join together in society, still there are probably not ten men in the country whose estimate of the Constitution they live under would be affected by these supererogatory objections. And if we are in any measure to grasp the office, dignity and authority of the Scriptures, we must not suppose we are dealing adequately with that lofty subject by exhausting thought and time in examining whether Moses either edited or wrote the Pentateuch just as it stands, or what was the book of the law found in the temple in the time of Josiah, or whether it is possible or likely that any changes of addition or omission may have crept into the text. If the most greedily destructive among all the theories of the modern critics (rather seriously at variance with one another) were established as true, it would not avail to impair the great facts of the history of man with respect to the Jews, and to the nations of the world; nor to disguise the light which those facts throw upon the pages of the Sacred Volume; nor to abate the commanding force with which, bathed, so to speak, in the flood of that light, the Bible invites, attracts, and commands the adhesion of mankind. Even the moral problems, which may be raised as to particular portions of the volume, and which may not have found any absolute and certain solution, are surely lost in the comprehensive contemplation of its general strain, its immeasurable loftiness of aim, and the vastness of the results which it, and its immediate accompaniments in institution and event, have wrought for our predecessors in the journey of life, for ourselves, and for the most forward, dominant, and responsible portions of our race.

In a passage which rises to the very highest level of British eloquence, Dr. Liddon,* exhausting all the resources of our language, has described, so far as man may describe it, the ineffable and unapproachable position held by the Sacred Volume. It is too long

---

* Sermon preached at St. Paul's on the Second Sunday in Advent, December 1889, pp. 28–31. [Since this was written, death has extinguished in Dr. Liddon a light of the English Church, singularly bright and pure.]

to quote, too special to appropriate; and to make extracts would only mangle it. The commanding eminence of the great preacher of our metropolitan Cathedral will fasten the public attention on the subject, and powerfully serve to show that the Scriptures, in their substantial tissue, rise far above the region of criticism, which shows no sign of being about to do anything permanent or effectual to lower their moral and spiritual grandeur, or to disguise or intercept their gigantic work.

I turn to a cognate topic. The impression prevails that, in this and other countries, the operative classes, as they are termed, have at the great centres of population, here and elsewhere, largely lost their hold upon the Christian creed. There may be exaggeration in this belief; but, all things taken together, there is evidently a degree of foundation for it. It does not mean, at least among us, that they have lost respect for the Christian religion, or for its ministers; or that they desire their children to be brought up otherwise than in the knowledge and practice of it; or that they themselves have snapped the last ties which, on the cardinal occasions of existence, associate them with its ordinances; or that they have renounced or modified the moral standards of conduct, which its conspicuous victory after an obstinate contest of many centuries, and its long possession of the social field, have established. It means no more, but also no less, than this, that their positive distinct acceptance of the articles of the Creed, and their sense of the dignity and value of the Sacred Record, are blunted, or in some cases even effaced.*

In passing I may be permitted to observe that if assent be more or less largely withheld by the less well-to-do segment of society, it is still, notwithstanding the sceptical movement of the day, very generally yielded in this country by the leisured and better provided classes in most, though not all, of their branches. I simply state this as fact, without drawing, in this case, any inference.

There seems thus to be, within certain limits, an approach to a reversal of the respective attitudes which prevailed in the infancy of our religion. Then the "poor" were the principal objects of the personal ministry of Christ Our Lord, and it was

* As I write in the general interests of belief, and on no narrower ground, it is with deep regret that I extract the following statement from the excellent compilation of Messrs. Macmillan, termed the *Statesman's Year-Book*, for 1890. In France account is taken at the census of religious belief, and in 1881, for the first time, a column was provided for those who declined to make any declaration of belief. The number of persons returned under this head is no less than 7,684,906.

their glory to be the readiest receivers of the Gospel. They were then, " the poor of this world, rich in faith, and heirs of the kingdom which He hath promised to them that love Him."* They had fewer obstacles, especially within themselves, to prevent their accepting the new religion. It was less hard for them to become "as little children." They had, to all appearance, more palpable interests in the promise of the life to come, as compared with the possession of the life that now is. The seeming change in their comparative facility of access to the Saviour, as respects belief, is one to afford much matter for meditation. The present purpose is to deal, in slight outline at least, with one of its causes. For one such cause certainly is the wide, though more or less vague disparagement of the Holy Scriptures recently observable in the surface currents of prevalent opinion, as regards their title to supply in a supreme degree food for the religious thought of man, and authoritative guidance for his life.

Amongst the suppositions, I believe erroneous, which tend to produce this disparagement are the following.

I. That the conclusions of science as to natural objects have shaken or destroyed

* James ii. 5.

the assertions of the early Scriptures with respect to the origin and history of the world, and of man, its principal inhabitant.

II. That their contents are in many cases offensive to the moral sense, and unworthy of an enlightened age.

III. That our race made its appearance in the world in a condition but one degree above that of the brute creation, and only by slow and painful but continual progress has brought itself up to the present level of its existence.

IV. That men have accomplished this by the exercise of their natural powers; and have never received the special teaching and authoritative guidance, which is signified under the name of Divine Revelation.

V. That the more considerable among the different races and nations of the world have devised, and established from time to time, their respective religions; and have in many cases accepted the promulgation of sacred books, which are to be considered as essentially of the same character with the Bible.

VI. That the books of the Bible, in many most important instances, and especially those books of the Old Testament which purport to be the earliest, so far from being contemporary with the events which they record, or with the authors to whom they are ascribed, are comparatively recent compilations from uncertain sources, and are therefore without authority.

Most of the foregoing remarks relate to the last of these assumptions; and I shall proceed to observe upon others among them.

There are propositions wider still, but wholly foreign to the present purpose; such as that God is essentially unknowable, that we have no reasonable evidence of a life beyond the grave, and that rational certainty is confined to material objects and to the testimony of the senses. Passing by these propositions, I confine myself wholly to what preceded them; and I shall endeavor, from some points of view, to present an opposing view of the spiritual field. Moreover, as each of these is the subject of a literature of its own which may be termed scientific, I here premise that what I have to say will, though I hope rational and true, be not systematic or complete, but popular and partial only; and will have for its immediate aim to show that there are grave reasons for questioning every really destructive proposition that has been advanced, and for withholding our assent from them until these reasons (and, as I conceive, many others) shall be confuted and set aside.

I shall, however, as being in duty bound to follow the truth so far as I can discern it, have to make many confessions in the course of my argument to the prejudice, not as I trust of Christian belief or of the Sacred Volume, but only of us, who as its students have failed gravely, and at many points, in the duty of a temperate and cautious treatment of it; as unhappily we have also failed, and often more grossly failed, in every other duty. But, as the lines and laws of duty at large remain unobscured, notwithstanding the imperfections everywhere diffused, so we may trust that sufficient light yet remains for us, if duly followed, whereby to establish the authority and sufficiency of Holy Scripture for its high moral and spiritual purposes. For the present, I have endeavored to point out that the operations of criticism properly so called, affecting as they do the literary form of the books, leave the questions of substance, namely, those of history, miracle, and revelation, substantially where they found them. I shall, in several succeeding papers, strive to show, at least by specimens, that science and research have done much to sustain the historical credit of the Old Testament: that in doing this they have added strength to the argument which contends that in them we find a

Divine revelation: and that the evidence, rationally viewed, both of contents and of results, binds us to stand where our forefathers have stood, upon the impregnable rock of Holy Scripture.

The Creation Story.

The Creation Story.

"The rising birth
Of Nature from the unapparent deep."
Par. Lost. B. vii.

IN recent controversies on the trustworthiness of the Scripture record, much has been thought to turn on the Creation Story ; and the special and separate importance thus attached to it has given it a separate and prominent position in the public view. This constitutes in itself a reason for addressing ourselves at once to the consideration of it, apart from any more general investigation touching either the older Scriptures at large, or any of the books which collectively compose them.

But there are broader and deeper reasons for this separate consideration. It is suggested, first, by the form which has been given to the relation itself. The narrative, given with wonderful succinctness in the first chapter of the Book of Genesis, and in the first three verses of the second chapter, stands distinct, in essential points, from all that follows in the Scriptures. It is a solitary and striking example of the detailed exposition of physical facts. For such an example we must suppose a purpose; and we have to inquire what that purpose was. Next, it seems as it were to trespass on the ground of science, and, independently of investigation and of evidence, to assert a rival authority. And further, forming no part, unless towards its close, of the history of man, and nowhere touching directly on human action, it severs itself from the rest of the Sacred Volume, and appears more as a preface to the history, than as a part of it.

And yet there are signs, in subsequent portions of the Volume, that this tale of the Creation was regarded by the Hebrews as both authoritative and important. For it gave form and shape to portions of their literature, in the central department of its devotions. Nay, traces of it may, perhaps, be found in the Book of Job (xxxviii.), where the Almighty challenges the patriarch on the primordial works of creation. More clearly in Psalm civ., where we have light, the firmament, the waters and their severance and confinement within bounds; a succession the same as in Genesis. Then follow mixedly the animal and vegetable creations, and man as the climax crowns the series in ver. 23. So in Psalm cxlviii. we have first (1-6) the heavens, the heavenly bodies, and the atmosphere; then, again mixedly, the earth and the agents affecting it, with the animate population (7-10), and lastly man. If there be some variation in the order of the details, still the idea of consecutive development, or evolution, which struck so forcibly the intelligence of Haeckel, is clearly impressed upon the whole. At a later date, and only (so far as is known) in the Greek tongue, we find a more nearly exact resemblance in the Song of the Three Children. The heavenly bodies and phenomena occupy the first division of the Song; then the earth is invoked to bless the Lord, with its mountains, vegetation, and waters; then the animate population of water, air, and land, in the order pursued in the first chapter of Genesis, and with the same remarkable omission of the great kingdom of the Reptiles at their proper place. Then follow the children of Men; and these fill the closing portion of the Song. The most noteworthy differences (which, however, are quite secondary, seem to be that there is no mention of the first beginnings of vegetation, and no supplemental notice, as in Gen. i. 24-30, of the reptiles.

But also the sun, moon, and stars, which

are categorically placed later in Genesis than vegetation, precede in the Song any notice of the earth. Let not this difference be hastily called a discrepancy. Each mode is to be explained by considering the character and purpose of the composition. In Genesis, it is a narrative of the action; in the Song, it is a panorama of the spectacle. Genesis, as a rule, refers each of the great factors of the visible world to its due order of origin in time; the Song enumerates the particulars as they are presented to the eye in a picture, where the transcendent eminence of the heavenly bodies as they are, and especially of the sun, gives to this group a proper priority.

But this Creation Story may have an importance for us even greater than it had for the Hebrews, or than it could have in any of those ages when all men believed, perhaps even too freely, in special modes of communication from the Deity to man, and had not a stock of courage or of audacity sufficient to question the possibility of a divine revelation. For we have now to bear in mind that the Book of Genesis generally contains a portion of human history, and that all human history is a record of human experience. It is not so with the introductory recital; for the contents of it lie outside of, and anterior to, the very earliest human experience. How came, then, this recital into the possession of a portion of mankind?

It is conceivable that a theory of Creation and of the ordering of the world might be bodied forth in poetry, or might under given circumstances be, as now, based on the researches of natural science.

But, in the first place, this recital cannot be due to the mere imagination of a poet. It is in a high degree, as we shall see, methodical and elaborate. And there is nothing either equalling or within many degrees approaching it, which can be set down to the account of poetry in other spheres of primitive antiquity, whatever their poetical opulence may have been. Further, the early Hebrews do not appear to have cultivated or developed any poetical faculty at all, except that which was exhibited in strictly religious work, such as the devotions of the Psalms, and (principally) the discourses and addresses of the Prophets.

As they were not, in a general sense, poetical, so neither were they in any sense scientific. By tradition, and by positive records, we know pretty well what kinds of knowledge were pursued in very early ages. They were most strictly practical. Take, for example, astronomy among the

Chaldees, or medicine among the Egyptians. The necessities of life then, as now, pressed upon man. We may say with much confidence that in remote antiquity there existed no science like geology, aiming to give a history of the earth. So, again, there was no cosmogony, professing to convey a history of the *kosmos* as then understood; which would have included, together with the earth, the sun, moon, planets, and atmosphere.

When, at a later date, speculation on physical origins began, it was rather on the primary idea than on any systematic arrangement or succession. With the Ionic, which was the earliest school of philosophy, the human intelligence was mainly busied in contending for one or other of the known material elements, as entitled to the honors of the primordial cause. Nor had even the Greeks or Romans formulated any scheme in any degree approaching that of Genesis for order and method, so late as the time when they became acquainted with the Hebrew Scriptures through their translation into Greek. The opening statement of Ovid in the "Metamorphoses" is remarkable; but at the time when he wrote, the Book of Genesis had been accessible to educated persons in what was then the chief literary language of the Romans. There is not, then, the smallest ground for treating the Mosaic cosmogony, whether in the way of original or copy, as the offspring of scientific inquiry.

To speak of it as guesswork would be irrational. There were no materials for guessing. There was no purpose to be served by guessing. For a record of the formation of the world we find no purpose in connection with the ordinary necessities or conveniences of life. Not to mention that down to this day there exists no cosmogony which can be called scientific, though there are theories both ingenious and beautiful, which apparently are coming to be more and more accepted; these, however, being of an origin decidedly late even in the history of modern physics.

But, further, as the Tale of Creation is not poetry nor is it science, so neither, according to its own aspect or profession, is it theory at all. The method here pursued is that of historical recital. The person, who composes or transmits it, seems to believe, and to intend others to believe, that he is dealing with matters of fact. But these matters of fact were, from the nature of the case, altogether inaccessible to inquiry, and impossible to attain by our ordinary mental faculties of perception or reflection, inasmuch as they date before the creation of our race. If it is, as it surely professes to be, a serious conveyance of truth, it can only be a communication from the Most High; a communication to man and for the use of man, therefore in a form adapted to his mind and to his use. If, thus considered, it is true, then it carries stamped upon it the proof of a Divine revelation; an assertion which cannot commonly be sustained from the nature of the contents as to this or that minute portion of Scripture at large.

If, when thus considered, it proves not to be true, we then have to consider what account of it we are in a condition to give. I cannot say that to me this appears an easy undertaking. "If," says Professor Dana with much reason, "it be true that the narration in Genesis has no support in natural science, it would have been better for its religious character that all the verses between the first and those on the creation of man had been omitted." *

But the truth, or trueness, of which I speak, is truth or trueness as conveyed to and comprehended by the mind of man; and, further, by the mind of man in a comparatively untrained and infant state. I cannot, indeed, wholly shut out from view the possibility that casual imperfections may

* "Creation." By Professor Dana. Oberlin, O., 1885; p. 202.

have crept into the record. Setting aside, however, that possibility, let us consider the conditions of the case as they are exhibited to us by reasonable likelihood; for, if the communication were divine, we may be certain that it would on that account be all the more strictly governed by the laws of the reasonable.

In an address * of singular ability on "The Discord and Harmony between Science and the Bible," Dr. Smith, of the University of Virginia, has drawn some very important distinctions. In the department of natural science, and in the department of Scriptural record, the question lies "between the present interpretation of certain parts of the Hebrew Scriptures, and the present interpretation of certain parts of nature." † "We must not too hastily assume that either of these interpretations is absolute and final." "The science of one epoch is to a large extent a help, which the science of the next uses and abandons." Dr. Smith points out as an example that, down to the early part of the present century, Newton's projectile theory of light seemed to be firmly established, but that it has given place to the theory of undulation, "which has now for fifty years reigned in its

* New York: Hatcham. The Address is dated July 27, 188-.   † *Ibid.* p. 3.

stead." Hence, he observes, we should not be too much elated by the discovery of harmonies, nor should we receive with impatience the assertion of contradictions. Throughout, it is probable, and not demonstrative, evidence with which we are dealing. There should always be a certain element of reserve in our judgments on particulars; yet probable evidence may come indefinitely near to demonstration; and, even as, while falling greatly short of it, it may morally bind us to action, so may it, on precisely the same principles, bind us to belief. What we have to do is, to deal with the evidence before us according to a rational appreciation of its force. It may show on this or that particular question the concord, or it may show the discord, between alleged facts of nature and alleged interpretations of Scripture; or it may leave the question open, for want of sufficient evidence, either way, on which to ground a conclusion.

It is by these principles, and under these limitations, that I desire to see the question tried in the terms in which I think it ought to be stated; namely, not whether the recitals in Genesis at each and every point have an accurately scientific form, but, Whether the statements of the Creation Story, as a whole, appear to stand in such a relation to the facts of natural science, so far as they have been ascertained, as to warrant or require our concluding that the statements have proceeded, in a manner above the ordinary manner, from the Author of the creation itself.*

Those, who maintain the affirmative of this proposition, have by opponents been termed Reconcilers; and it is convenient, in a controverted matter, to have the power of reference by a single word to the proposers of any given opinion. The same rule of convenience may perhaps justify me in designating those who would assert the negative by the name of Contradictionists. The recorder of the Creation Story in Genesis I may designate by the name of Moses himself, or the Mosaist, or the Mosaic writer. This would not be reasonable, if there were anything extravagant in the supposition that there is a groundwork of fact for the tradition which treats Moses as the author of the Pentateuch. But such a supposition, in whole or in part, is sustained by

---

* See the attractive paper of Professor Pritchard, in his "Occasional Thoughts," Murray, 1889. He says on p. 261, "I cannot accept the Proem as being, or even as intended to be, an exact and scientific account of Creation," but adds that it "contains within it elements of that same sort of *superhuman aid or superintendence, which is generally understood by the undefined term of inspiration.*"

many and strong presumptions, and I bear in mind that Wellhausen, in giving Bleek's "Introduction" to the world, stated it as his opinion that there is a strong Mosaic element in the Pentateuch.

It does not seem too much to say, that the conveyance of scientific instruction as such would not, under the circumstances of the case, be a reasonable object for the Mosaic writer to pursue; for the condition of primitive man, as it is portrayed in the Book of Genesis, did not require, perhaps did not admit of, scientific instruction. On the other hand, it could not but be a reasonable object then to convey to the mind of man, such as he actually was, a moral lesson drawn from and founded on that picture, that assemblage of created objects, which was before his eyes, and with which he lived in perpetual contact. We have, indeed, to consider both what lesson it would be most rational to convey, and by what method it would be most rational to stamp it, as a living lesson, on the mind by which it was to be received. And the question finally to be decided is not, whether according to the present state of knowledge the recital in the Book of Genesis is at each several point either precise or complete. It may here be general, there particular; it may here describe a continuous process, and it may there make large omissions, if the things omitted were either absolutely or comparatively immaterial to its purpose ; it may be careful of the actual succession in time, or may deviate from it, according as the one or the other best subserved the general and principal aim ; so that the true question, I must repeat, is no more than this: Do the propositions of the Creation Story in Genesis appear to stand in such a relation to the facts of natural science, so far as they are ascertained, as to warrant or require our concluding that these propositions proceeded, in a manner above the ordinary manner, from the Author of the visible creation?

What, then, may we conceive to have been the moral and spiritual lessons which the Mosaist had to communicate, and not only to communicate but to infuse or to impress? I do not presume to attempt an exhaustive enumeration. But it is not difficult to specify a variety of purposes which the narrative was calculated to promote, and which were of great and obvious value for the education of mankind.

First, it was fitted to teach man his proper place in creation in relation to its several orders, and thereby to prepare at least for the formation of the idea of relative duty, as between man and other created beings.

Secondly, it presented to his mind, and by means of detail made him know and feel what was the beautiful and noble home that he inhabited, and with what a fatherly and tender care Providence had prepared it for him to dwell in. There was a picture before his eyes. That picture was filled with objects of nature, animate and inanimate. I say, one of its great aims may have been to make him know and feel by means of detail; for wholesale teaching, teaching in the lump, or abstract teaching, mostly ineffective even now, would have been wholly futile then. It was needful to use the simplest phrases, that the primitive man might receive a conception, thoroughly faithful in broad outline, of what his Maker had been about on his behalf. So the Maker condescends to partition and set out His work, in making it a picture.

But He proceeds further (and this is the climax) to represent Himself as resting after it. This declaration is in no conflict with any scientific record. It, however, implies a license in the use of language, which for its boldness was never exceeded in any interpretation, reconciling or other, which has been applied to any part of the text of Genesis. But it draws its ample warrant from the strong educative lesson that is to be learned from it; for it invests both with majesty and authority the doctrine of a day of rest, which was of the highest importance to the higher and inner life of man, and which the daily cares of his existence were but too likely, as experience proved, to efface from his recollection.

I contend then, thirdly, that the Creation Story was intended to have a special bearing on the great institution of the day of rest, or Sabbath, by exhibiting it in the manner of an object lesson. Paley, indeed, has said that God blessed the seventh day and sanctified it (Gen. ii. 3), not at that time but for that reason. He is a writer much to be respected, for many reasons; but, in dealing with Holy Scripture, he was somewhat apt to rest upon the surface. And now we have learned from Assyrian researches how many and how sharply traced are the vestiges, long anterior to the delivery of the law, of some early institution or command, which in that region evidently had given a special sanctity to the number seven, and, in particular, to the seventh day.

Man then, childlike and sinless, had to receive a lesson which was capable of gradual development, and which spoke to something like the following effect. It has not been by a slight or single effort that the nature, in which you are moulded, has been lifted to its present level; you have reached it by steps and degrees, and by a plan which, stated in rough outline, may stir your faculties, and help them onwards to the truth through the genial action of wonder, delight, and gratitude. This was a lesson, as it seems to me, perhaps quite large enough for the primitive man on the facts of creation, and one which, when he had heard and had begun to digest it, might well be followed by a rest for generations.

And it further seems to have been vital to the efficiency of this lesson, from such a point of view, that it should have been sharply broken up into parts, although there might be in nature nothing, at any precise points of breakage or transition, to correspond physically with those divisions. They would become intelligible, significant, and useful on a comparison of the several processes in their developed state, and of the vast and measureless differences, which in that state they severally present to contemplation. As, when a series of scenes are now made to move along before the eye of a spectator, his attention is not fixed upon the joints which divide them, but on the scenes themselves, yet the joints constitute a framework as it were for each, and the idea of each is made more distinct and lively than it would have been if, without any note of division, they had run into one another.

There is, however, another purpose, not yet named, and more remote yet perhaps even more vital, which appears to be powerfully served by the Creation Story of the Bible. In the prehistoric time, polytheism was very largely engendered by national distinctions, rivalries, and amalgamations. By a ready and ingenious compromise each people became habituated to recognize a deity all-sufficient for its own wants, but unconcerned with those of others. In the course of time and of successive change, many of these deities might find themselves inducted into one and the same thearchy, or mythological system, such as that of Assyria or of Olympus, and sitting there side by side. When this happened, the polytheistic idea had reached its full development. But the road to it lay principally through the erection of separate thrones each for its particular national organization, and through the limits thus imposed upon the earlier and more proper conception of a Divine Governor. But where the Creation Story of Genesis was received, the door was effectually closed for all thinking men against these coequal and purely national gods. And how? Because the God of Israel was the Maker of the world, and of all the nations in it. It was His creation; and its inhabitants, whether terrestrial or celestial, were His creatures. Thus the narrative in this great chapter was nothing less than a charter of monotheism; and though, in Israelitish practice, Baal and Ashtoreth might find their way into popular worship, and spread around them an infinity of corruption, the lines of the dogma never were obscured, and the standard of authoritative reform still lifted up its head to heaven from the first day of idolatry to the last, when, in the Exile, it was finally submerged.*

How effectually and vividly this great idea of creation, lost or dilapidated elsewhere, was impressed upon the Hebrew mind we may perceive from an usage in the Psalms, to which I do not remember a parallel in the classical literature. The lower orders of animated creatures are themselves placed in a living relation to the Almighty. "The lions roaring after their prey, do seek their meat from God. . . . . These all wait upon thee; that thou mayest give them meat in due season." † Nor is the boldness of Hebrew devotion arrested at this point. It extends to the inanimate

---

* For the further elucidation of the subject of this paragraph see the Postscript to " The Creation Story."
† Ps. civ. 21, 27.

world. "The heavens declare the glory of God; and the firmament showeth His handiwork. . . . . Their sound is gone out into all lands, and their words into the ends of the world. . . . . The sun cometh forth as a bridegroom out of his chamber, and rejoiceth as a giant to run his course." * This is without doubt noble poetry, but it is also nobler than any poetry. Mute Nature is instinct and vocal with worship, and Creation in its humblest orders, giving a lesson to its loftiest, ministers to the glory of the Most High.

In order, then, to approach any attempt at comparison between the record of Scripture and the record of Natural Science, we must consider first, as far as reasonable presumption carries us, what is the proper object of the scientist, and what was the proper object of Moses, or of the Mosaic writer, in the first chapter of Genesis.

The object of the scientist is simply to state the facts of nature in the cosmogony as and so far as he can find them. The object of the Mosaic writer is broadly distinct; it is, surely, to convey moral and spiritual training. This training was to be conveyed to human beings of childlike temperament and of unimproved understanding. It was his business to use those words which

* Ps. xix. 1–5.

would best convey the lessons he had to teach; which would carry *most truth* into the minds of those he taught. This observation has not the honors of originality. "He emphasized," says Rabbi Grossmann,* in his interesting tract on Maimonides, "as very proper and wise, the Talmudic maxim, that the Torah employs such diction as is likely to be most communicative."

In speaking of the Mosaic writer, I would, without presumption, seek to include any divine impulse which may have prompted him, or may have dictated any communication from God to man, in whatever form it may have been conveyed. With this aim in view, words of figure, though literally untrue, might carry more truth home than words of fact; and words less exact will even now often carry more truth than words superior in exactness. The truth to be conveyed was, indeed, in its basis physical; but it was to serve moral and spiritual ends, and accordingly by these ends the method of its conveyance behoved to be shaped and pictured.

I submit, then, that the days of creation are neither the solar days of twenty-four hours, nor are they the geological periods which the geologist himself is compelled popularly, and in a manner utterly remote

* P. 12. Putnam, New York and London, 1890.

from precision, to describe as millions upon millions of years. To use such language as this is simply to tell us, that we have no means of forming a determinate idea upon the subject of the geologic periods. I set aside both these interpretations, as I do not think the Mosaist intended to convey an idea like the first, which was false, or like the second, which for his auditory would have been barren and unmeaning. Unmeaning, and even confusing in the highest degree; for large statements in figures are well known to be utterly beyond comprehension for man at an early intellectual stage; and I have myself, I think, shown * that, even among the Achaian or Homeric Greeks, the limits of numerical comprehension were extremely narrow, and all large numbers were used, so to speak, at a venture.

It seems to me that the "days" of the Mosaist are more properly to be described as CHAPTERS IN THE HISTORY OF THE CREATION. That is to say, the purpose of the writer, in speaking of the days, was the same as the purpose of the historian is, when he divides his work into chapters. His object is to give clear and sound instruction. So that he can do this, and in

---

* "Studies on Homer and the Homeric Age," vol. iii., Section on Number.

order that he may do it, the periods of time assigned to each chapter are longer or shorter, according as the one or the other may minister to better comprehension of his subject by his readers. Further, in point of chronology, his chapters often overlap. He finds it needful, always keeping his end in view, to pursue some narrative to its close, and then, stepping backwards, to take up some other series of facts, although their exordium dated at a period of time which he has already traversed. The resources of the literary art, aided for the last four centuries by printing, enable the modern writer to confront more easily these difficulties of arrangement, and so to present the material to his reader's eye, in text or margin, as to place the texture of his chronology in harmony with the texture of the action he has to relate. The Mosaist, in his endeavor to expound the ordinary development of the visible world, had no such resources. His expedient was to lay hold on that which, to the mind of his time, was the best example of complete and orderly division. This was the day; an idea at once simple, definite, and familiar. As one day is divided from another, not by any change visible to the eye at a given moment, yet effectually, by the broad chasm of the intervening night, so were the stages of the creative work several and distinct, even if, like the lapse of time, they were without breach of continuity. Each had its work, each had the beginning and the completion of that work, even as the day is begun by its morning, and completed and concluded by its evening.

And now to sum up. In order that the narrative might be intelligible, it was useful to subdivide the work. This could most effectively be done by subdividing it into periods of time. And further, it was well to choose that particular circumscription or period of time which is the most definite and best understood. Of all these, the day is clearly the best, as compared with the month or the year—first, because of its small and familiar compass; and, secondly, because of the strong and marked division which separates one day from another.

Hence, we may reasonably argue, it is that not here only, but throughout the Scripture, and even down to the present time in familiar human speech, the day is figuratively used to describe periods of time, perfectly undefined as such, but defined, for practical purposes, by the lives or events to which reference is made. And if it be said there was a danger of its being misunderstood in this particular case, the answer is that such danger of misapprehension attaches in various degrees to all use of figurative language; but figurative language is still used. And with reason because the mischiefs arising from such danger are rare and trivial, in comparison with the force and clearness which it lends to truth on its passage, through a clouded atmosphere of folly, indifference, and prejudice, into the mind of man. In this particular case, the danger and inconvenience are at their minimum, the benefit at its zenith; for no moral mischief ensues because some have supposed the days of the creation to be pure solar days of twenty-four hours, while the benefit has been that the grand conception of orderly development, and ascent from chaos to man, became among the Hebrew people an universal and familiar truth, of which other races appear to have lost sight.

I may now part from the important and long-vexed discussion on the Mosiac days. But I shall further examine the general question, what is the true method, what the reasonable spirit, of interpretation to be applied to the words of the Creation Story? I will state frankly my opinion that, in this important matter, too much has sometimes been conceded in modern days to the Scientist and to the Hebraist, just as in former days too much was allowed to the unproved assumptions of the Theologian. Now it is evident that the proper ground of the Scientist and of the Hebraist respectively is unassailable, as against those who are neither Scientists nor Hebraists. On the meaning of the words used in the Creation Story I, as an *ignoramus*, have only to accept the statements of Hebrew scholars, with gratitude for the aid received; and in like manner those of men skilled in natural science on the nature and succession of the orders of being, and the transitions from one to the other. Not that their statements are inerrable; but they constitute the best working material in our possession. Still they are the statements of men whose title to speak with authority is confined to their special province; and if we allow them without protest to go beyond it, and still to claim that authority when they are what is called at school "out of bounds," we are much to blame, and may suffer for our carelessness.

I will now endeavor to illustrate and apply what has been said. The Hebraist says, I will conduct you safely (as far as the case allows) to the meaning of the Hebrew words. And the Scientist makes the same promise in regard to the facts of the created orders, so far as they are exhibited by geological investigations into the crust of the earth. At first sight it may seem as if these two authoritative witnesses must cover the whole ground, each setting out from his own point of departure, the two then meeting in the midst, and leaving no unoccupied space between them. But my contention is that there is a ground which neither of them is entitled to occupy in his character as a specialist, and on which he has no warrant for entering, except in so far as he is a just observer and reasoner in a much wider field. And what is the residuary subject-matter still to be disposed of? Not the meaning of the Hebrew words. The Hebraist has already given us their true equivalents in English. We now learn, for example, that the "whales" of Gen. i. 21 are not whales at all, but that they are aquatic monsters* or great creatures; while we learn from the biologist that the whale is a late mammal. So geology has acquainted us what are the relative dates of the water and of the land populations, and has supplied much information as to reptiles, birds,

* R. V., the great sea-monsters. "It seems, on the whole, most probable, that the creatures here said to have been created were serpents, crocodiles, and other huge saurians, though possibly any large monsters of sea or river may be included" (Bp. Browne *in loc.*, "Speaker's Commentary"). Possibly a word meaning, whether wholly or *inter alia*, crocodiles would convey a pretty clear idea to the mind of the Hebrews, after their sojourn in Egypt.

and beasts. But there remains a great uncovered ground, and a great unsolved question. It is this. Given the facts as the geologist is led to state them, given the Hebrew tongue as the instrument through which the relator has to work, what are the terms, and what is the order and adjustment of terms, through which he can convey most of truth and force, with least of incumbrance and of impediment, to the mind of man, in the condition in which he had to deal with it? Let me be permitted to say that the only specialism, which can be of the smallest value here, is that of the close observer of human nature; of the student of human action, and of the methods which Divine Providence employs in the conduct of its dealings with men. Certainly I can lay no claim to be heard here more than any other person. Yet will I say, that any man whose labor and duty for several scores of years has included as their central point the study of the means of making himself intelligible to the mass of men, is *pro tanto* perhaps in a better position to judge what would be the forms and methods of speech proper for the Mosaic writer to adopt, than the most perfect Hebraist as such, or the most consummate votary of natural sciences as such.

I will now endeavor to try some portions of the case which turn upon verbal difficulty. At the outset of the narrative the relator says, that "the earth was without form and void" (Gen. i. 2) and that "the spirit of God moved upon the face of the waters." Nay, how is this, says the Hebraist? The Hebrew word for earth means earth, and the word used for water never means anything except water. But according to the beautiful theory, which has during the last half-century won so largely the adhesion of the scientific world, and which seems to be mainly called the nebular theory, at the commencement of the process which Genesis describes, and in its early stages, there was no earth, and there were no waters. Is the relator here really at fault? It seems to me that it might be quite as easy to cavil at the phrase nebular theory, though it be one in use among scientific men, as it is to find fault with these words of Genesis. For nothing can be more different than a *nebula* or cloud from a vast expanse of incandescent gaseous matter. In truth, we seem to have for our point of departure a time when all the elements and all the forces of the visible universe were in chaotic mixture, whereas there could hardly be any sort of *nebula* until they had begun to be disengaged from one another. How then are we to judge of the use of the word "earth" by the Mosaic writer? Is it not thus? He is dealing with an Adam, or with a primitive race of men, who have the earth under their eyes. He wants to give them an idea of its coming into existence. And he says what we may fairly paraphrase in this way: that which has now become earth, and was then becoming earth, the solid well-defined form you see, was as yet without form and void; epithets which I am told might be improved upon, but this is a matter by the way.

So again with respect to water. The men for whom the relator wrote knew, perhaps, of no fluid except water, at any rate of none vast and practically measureless in volume. What was the idea he had to convey? It was not the special and distinctive character of the liquid called water; it was the broad separation between solid as such, familiar, firm, immovable under his feet, and fluid as such, movable and fluctuating at large in space. No doubt the idea conveyed by the word waters is an imperfect idea, although waters are still waters at times when they may be holding vast quantities of solid in solution. But it was an idea easy, clear, and familiar up to the point of expressing forcibly the contrast between the ancient state of things, with its weltering waste, and the recent and defined conditions of the habitable earth. Could we ask of the relator more than that he should employ, among the words at his disposal, that which would come nearest to conveying a true idea? And had he any word so good as water for his purpose, though it was but an approximation to the actual fact? Dr. Driver describes the scene as that of a "surging chaos." An admirable phrase, I make no doubt, for our modern and cultivated minds; but a phrase which, in my judgment, would have left the pupils of the Mosaic writer exactly in the condition out of which it was his purpose to bring them; namely, a state of utter ignorance and total darkness, with possibly a little ruffle of bewilderment to boot. Another description claiming high authority is, an "uncompounded, homogeneous, gaseous condition" of matter; to which the same observation will apply. Even now, it is only by rude and bald approximations that the practised intellects of our scientists can bring home to us a conception of the actual process by which *chaos* passed into *kosmos*, or, in other words, confusion became order, medley became sequence, seeming anarchy became majestic law, and horror softened into beauty. Before censuring the Mosaist, who had to deal with grown children, let the adverse critic try his hand upon some little child. I believe he will find that the method and language of this relator are not only good, but superlatively good, for the aim he had in view, if once for all we get rid of standards of interpretation other than the genuine and just one, which tests the means employed by their relation to the end contemplated and sought.

I now approach a larger head of objection, which is usually handled by the Contradictionists in a tone of confidence rising into the pæan of triumph. But let me, before presuming to touch on objections to particulars of the Creation Story, guard myself against being supposed to put forward any portion of what follows as unconditional assertion, or final comment on the text. The general situation is this. Objectors do not hesitate to declare dogmatically that the Great Chapter is in contradiction with the laws and facts of nature, and that attempts to reconcile them are futile and irrational. It is thus sought to close the question. My aim is to show that the question is not closed, and that the condemnation pronounced upon the Mosaist is premature. For this purpose I offer conjecturally, and in absolute submission to all that biology and geology, or other forms of science, have established, replies which are strictly provisional; but replies which I consider that the Contradictionist ought, together with other and weightier replies, to confute, or legitimately to consider, before he can be warranted in asserting the contradiction. But I proceed.

How hopeless, is the cry, to reconcile Genesis with fact, when, as a fact, the sun is the source of light, and yet in Genesis, light is the work of the first day, and vegetation of the third, while sun, moon, and stars appear only on the fourth! Nay, worse still. Whereas the morning and the evening depend wholly on the rotation of the earth upon its own axis as it travels round the sun, the Mosaist is so ignorant that he gives us not days only, but the mornings and the evenings of days before the sun is created. And so his narration explodes, not by blows aimed at it from without, but by its own internal self-contradictions. It is hissed, like a blundering witness, out of court. Not that this is the opinion of astronomers in general. Mr. Lockyer,* for example, cites with apparent approval a passage from his very distinguished predecessor in the science, Halley, who says that the diffused lucid medium he had found disposed of the diffi-

* *Nineteenth Century*, Nov. 1889, p. 788.

culty which some have moved against the description Moses gives of the Creation, alleging that light could not be created without the sun.

The first triad of days, says Professor Dana,* sets forth the events connected with the inorganic history of the earth. The second triad, from the fourth day to the sixth, is occupied with the events of the organic history, from the creation of the first animal to man. He finds in the general structure of the narrative a considerable degree of elaboration, an arrangement full of art. The passage from ver. 14 to ver. 19 is, in one sense, a qualification of the order he thinks to have been laid down, inasmuch as the heavenly bodies belong to the inorganic division of the history. From another point of view, however, this arrangement contributes in a marked manner to the symmetry of the narrative. The first triad of days begins with the first and gradual detachment of light from the "surging chaos"; the second, at the stage in which light has reached its final distribution. The central mass had now assumed with a certain amount of regularity (for according to heliologists the process does not even yet appear to be absolutely completed) its spherical and luminous figure, after shedding off

* Dana's "Creation," p. 207.

from itself the minor masses, each to find for itself its own orbit of rotation. Or, if we are to assume that the photosphere or vapor-envelope of the earth itself had obstructed the vision of the sun, we have, further, to assume * that this obstacle had now disappeared, and the visibility of the sun was established. So that light, or the light-power, while diffused, ushers in the first division of the mighty process; the same light-power, concentrated by the operation of the rotatory principle, and for practical purposes become such as we now know it, is placed at the head of the second division, the division that deals with organic life.

It is remarkable, that the subject of light is the only one which is dealt with in two separate sections of the narrative. The gradual severance, or disengagement, of the earth from its present vesture, the atmosphere, and of the solid land from the ocean, are continuously handled in verses 6–10. Each of the processes is summed up into its grand result, as if it had been a violent, convulsive, instantaneous act. The avoidance of all attempt to explain the process seems to me only a proof of the wisdom which guided the formation of the tale. To the primitive man it would have become a

* Guyot, "Creation," ch. xi. p. 92.

barren puzzle; the wood must have been lost in the trees. As it now stands, mental confusion is avoided, and definite ideas are conveyed.

There seems, however, to be a special reason for the introduction of the heavenly bodies at this particular place. It was evidently needful at some place or other to give a specific account of the day, or compartment of time, which is employed to mark the severance of the different stages of creation from each other. At what point of the narrative could this account be most properly and most accurately introduced? In order to answer this question, let us consider the situation rather more at large.

The supposition is, that we set out with a seething mass that contains all the elements which are to become the solids and liquids, the moist and dry, the heat and the non-heat or cold, the light and the non-light or darkness, that so largely determine the external conditions of our present existence. By degrees, as, according to the rarity or density of parts, the centripetal or the centrifugal force prevails, the huge bulk of the sun consolidates itself in the centre, and aggregations of matter (rings, according to Guyot,* which afterwards become, or may become, spheres), are detached from it to

* "Creation," pp. 67, 73.

form the planets, under the agency of the same mechanical forces; all or some of them, in their turn, dismissing from their as yet ill-compacted surfaces other subaltern masses to revolve around them as satellites, or otherwise, according to the balance of forces, to take their course in space. Meantime, the great cooling process, which is still in progress at this day, has begun. It proceeds at a rate determined for it by its particular conditions, among which mass and motion are of essential consequence; for, other things being equal, a small body will cool faster and a large body will cool slower; and a body moving more rapidly through space of a lower temperature than its own will cool more rapidly; while one which is stationary, or more nearly stationary, or which diffuses heat less rapidly from its surface into the colder space, will retain a high temperature longer. Owing to these perhaps with other causes, the temperature of the earth-surface has been adapted to the conditions of human life, and of the more recent animal life, for a very long time; to those of the earlier animals, and of vegetation in its different orders, for we know not how much longer; while the sun, though gradually losing some part of his stock of caloric, still remains at a temperature inordinately high, and with a formation comparatively incomplete.

Considering, then, what are the relations between the conditions of heat and those of moisture, and how the coatings of vapor, "the swaddling-band of cloud,"* might affect the visibility of bodies, may it not be rash to affirm that the sun is, as a definite and compact body, older than the earth? or that it is so old? or that the Mosaist might not properly treat the visibility of the sun, in its present form, as best marking for man the practical inception of his existence? or that, with heat, light, soil, and moisture ready to its service, primordial vegetation might not exist on the surface of a planet like the earth, before the sun had fully reached his matured condition of sufficiently compact, material, and well-defined figure, and of visibility to the eye? May not, once for all, the establishment of the relation of visibility between earth and sun be the most suitable point for the relator in Genesis to bring the two into connection? And here again I would remind the reader that the Mosaic days may be chapters in a history; and that, not in despite of the law of series, but with a view to its best practicable application, the chapters of a history may overlap.

The priority of Earth to Sun, as given in

* Dana, p. 210.

the narrative, carries us so far as this, **that vegetative work** (of what kind I shall presently inquire) **is stated to be proceeding on the surface of the earth before any relation of earth with sun is declared.** It is then declared in the terms, "and God *made* two great lights" (ver. 16). Now the *making* of earth is nowhere declared, but only implied. And who shall say that there is some one exact point of time in the continuous process which (according to the nebular theory) reaches from the first beginning of rotation down to the present condition of the solar system, to which point, and to which alone, the term making must belong? But, unless there be such a point, it seems very difficult to convict the Mosaic writer of error in the choice he has made of an opportunity for introducing the heavenly bodies into his narrative.

I suppose that no apology is needed for his mentioning the moon and the stars as accessories in the train of the sun, and combining them all without note of time, although their several "makings" may have proceeded at different speeds. But here again we find exhibited that principle of relativity to man and his uses, by which the writer in Genesis appears so wisely to steer his course throughout. We are told of "two great lights" (ver. 16); and one of them is the moon. The formation of the stars is interjected soon after, as if comparatively insignificant. But the planet-stars individually are in themselves far greater and more significant than the moon, which is denominated a great light. In what sense is the moon a great light? Only in virtue of its relation to us. For its magnitude, as it is represented on the human retina, is far larger than that of the stars, approaching that of the sun; and its office also makes it the queen of the nocturnal heaven. So, then, the general upshot is, that the mention of the sun is introduced at that point in the cosmogonic process when, from the condition of our form and atmosphere, or of his, or of both, he had become so definite and visible as to be finally efficient for his office of dividing day from day, and year from year; that the planets, being of an altogether secondary importance to us, simply appear as his attendant company; and that to the moon, a body in itself comparatively insignificant, is awarded a rather conspicuous place, which, if objectively considered, is out of proportion, but which at once falls into line when we acknowledge relativity as the basis of the narrative, by reason of the great importance of the functions, which this satellite discharges on behalf of the inhabitants of the earth.

Next, it is alleged that we have days with an evening and a morning before we have a sun to supply a measure of time for them. Doubtless there could be no approach to anything like an evening and a morning, so long as light was uniformly diffused. But under the nebular theory, the work of the first day implies an initial concentration of light; and, from the time when light began to be thus powerfully concentrated, would there not be an evening and a morning, though imperfect, for any revolving solid of the system, according as it might be turned towards, or from, the centre of the highest luminosity?

But we have not yet emerged from the net of the Contradictionist, who lays hold on the vegetation verses (11, 12) to impeach the credit of the Creation Story. The objection here becomes twofold. First, we have vegetation anterior to the sun; and secondly, this is not merely an aquatic vegetation for the support of aquatic life, nor merely a rude and primordial vegetation, such as that of and before the coal-measures, but a vegetation complete and absolute, including fern-grass, then the herb yielding seed, and lastly the fruit-tree, yielding fruit after its kind, whose seed is in itself. Here is the food of mammals and even of man provided, when neither of them was created, or was even about to exist until after many a long antecedent stage of lower life had found its way into creation and undertaken its office there.

First, as regards vegetation before the sun's performance of his present function in the heavens is announced. There were light and heat, atmosphere with its conditions of moist and dry, soil prepared to do its work in nutrition. Can there be ground for saying that, with such provision made, vegetation could not, would not, take place? Let us, for argument's sake, suppose that the sun could now recede into an earlier condition, could go back by some few stages of that process through which he became our sun; his material less compact, his form less defined, his rays more intercepted by the " swaddling-band " of cloud and vapor. Vegetation might be modified in character, but must it therefore cease? May we not say that a far more violent paradox would have been hazarded, and a sounder objection would have lain, had the Mosaic writer failed to present to us at least an initial vegetation before the era at which the sun had obtained his present degree of definiteness in spherical form, and the conditions for the transmission of his rays to us had reached substantially their present state?

But, then, it is fairly observed that the

vegetation as described is not preparatory and initial, but full-formed; also, that any tracing of vegetation anterior to animal life in the strata is ambiguous and obscure. In the age of Protozoa, the earliest living creatures, the indications of plants are not determinable, according to the high authority of Sir J. W. Dawson. It is observed by Canon Driver " that the proof from science of the existence of plants before animals is inferential and *à priori.*" * Guyot, however, holds a directly contrary opinion, and says the present remains indicate a large presence of infusorial protophytes in the early seas.† But suppose the point to be conceded. Undoubtedly, all *à priori* assumptions ought in inquiries of this kind to be watched with the utmost vigilance and jealousy. Still there are limits, beyond which vigilance and jealousy cannot push their claims. Is there anything strange in the supposition that the comparatively delicate composition of the first vegetable structures should have given way, and become indiscernible to us, amidst the shock and pressure of firmer and more durable material? The flesh of the mammoth has, indeed, been preserved to us, and eaten by dogs

---

* " The Cosmogony of Genesis," in *The Expositor*, January 1886, p. 29.
† " Creation," x. p. 90.

in our own time, though coming down from ages which we have no means of measuring; but then it was not exposed to the same pressure, and it subsisted under conditions of temperature which were adequately antiseptic. But has all palæozoic life been ascertained by its flesh, or do we not owe our knowledge of many among the earlier forms of animated life altogether to their osseous structures? And, in cases where only bone remains, is it an extravagant use of argument *à priori* to hold that there must have been flesh also? And, if flesh, why should not vegetable matter have subsisted, and have disappeared? Canon Driver, indeed, observes * that from a very early date animals preyed upon animals. Still the first animal could not prey upon himself; there must have been vegetable *pabulum*, out of which an animal body was first developed. "Before the beasts," says Sir George Stokes, "came the plants, plants which are necessary for their sustenance."†

Next, with respect to the objection that the vegetation of the eleventh and twelfth verses is a perfected vegetation, and that there existed no such vegetation before animal life began. But why are we to sup-

* *The Expositor*, January, 1886, p. 29.
† Letter to Mr. Elflein, Aug. 14, 1883.

pose that the Mosaic writer intended to say that such a vegetation did exist before animal life began? For no other reason than this: having mentioned the first introduction of vegetable life, he carries it on, without breaking his narrative, to its completion. In so proceeding, he does exactly what the historian does when, for the sake of clearer comprehension, he brings one series of events from its inception to its close, although in order of time the beginning only, and not the completion, belongs to the epoch at which he introduces it. What I have called the rule of relativity, the intention, namely, to be intelligible to man, seems to show the reason of his arrangement. If his meaning was, "The beautiful order of trees, plants, and grasses which you see around you had its first beginnings in the era when living creatures were about to commence their movements in the waters and on the earth, and all this was part of the fatherly work of God on your behalf"—such meaning was surely well expressed, expressed after a sound and workmanlike fashion, in the text of the Creation Story as it stands.

I will next notice the objection that the Mosaic writer takes (according to the received version) no notice of the great age of reptiles, but proceeds at once from the creation of marine animals (ver. 20) to the fowl that may "fly above the earth in the open firmament of heaven." He thus passes over without notice the amphibians, the reptiles proper, the insects, and the marsupial or early mammals, on his way to the birds. It is added that he brackets the birds with the fishes, and thus makes them of the same date.

It is requisite here to observe, with respect to birds, that Professor Dana * writes of the narrative in Genesis as follows: speaking of the relation between the Mosaic narrative and the ascertained facts of science, he uses these words: "The accordance is exact with the succession made out for the earliest species of these grand divisions, if we except the division of birds, about which there is doubt."

Owen, however, in his " Palæontology," † places animal life in six classes, according to the following order, namely—

1. Invertebrates.
2. Fishes.
3. Reptiles.
4. Birds.
5. Mammals.
6. Man.

In the more recent "Manual" of Profes-

---

* "Creation," as before, p. 215.
† Second edition, 1861, p. 5.

sor Prestwich (1886) the order of seniority stands as follows:—

1. Cryptogamous Plants.
2. Fishes.
3. Birds.
4. Mammals.
5. Man.

In the "Manual"* of Etheridge we are supplied with the following series, after fishes: 1. Fossil reptiles. 2. Ornithosauria; "*flying animals, which combined the character of reptiles with those of birds.*" 3. The first birds of the secondary rocks, with "feathers in all respects similar to those of existing birds." 4. Mammals.

It thus appears that much turns on the definition of a bird, and that, in this point as in others, it is hard, on the evidence thus presented, seriously to impeach the character of the Creation Story. Largely viewed, the place of birds, as an order in creation, is given us by our scientific teachers, or, as I have shown, by many and recognized authorities among them, between fishes and the class of mammals. It is a gratuitous assumption that the Mosaist intends to assign to them the same date as fishes; he places them in the same day, but then we have to bear in mind that he more than once gives several actions to the same

* Phillips's "Manual of Geology," part ii., by R. Etheridge, F. R. S., chap. xxv. pp. 511-520.

day. He sets them after the fishes; and the fairer construction surely is, not that they were contemporaneous, but that they were subsequent. He forbears, it is true, to notice amphibious reptiles, insects, and marsupials. And why? All these, variously important in themselves, fill no large place, some of them no place at all, in the view and in the concerns of primitive man; and, having man for his object, he forbears, on his guiding principle of relativity, to incumber his narrative with them.

If it be true that the demarcation of the order of birds in creation is less sharply drawn than that (for example) of fishes and of mammals, may we not be permitted to trace a singular propriety in the diminution, so to speak, of emphasis with which the Mosaist gives to their introduction a more qualified distinctness of outline, by simply subjoining them (ver. 20) to the aquatic creation.

I have now made bold to touch on the principal objections popularly known. They run into details which it has not been possible fully to notice, but which seem to be without force, except such as they derive from the illegitimate process of holding down the Mosaic writer in his narration, so short, so simple, so sublime, by restraints which the ordinary historian, though he has plenty of auxiliary expedients, and is under no restraint of space, finds himself obliged to shake off if he wishes to be understood. On the introduction of the great or recent mammals, and of man, as the objector is silent, I remain silent also.

It would be uncandid, however, not to notice the "creeping thing" of verses 24, 25, and 26. In these verses the "creeping thing" is distinguished from cattle, and undoubtedly appears upon the scene as if it were a formation wholly new. If the Mosaist really intended to convey that this was the first appearance of the creeping thing in creation, there is I suppose no doubt that he is at war with the firmly established witness of natural science. Guyot, indeed, says* that these creeping things are not reptiles, but are the smaller mammals, rats, mice, and the like. If, however, the common rendering be maintained, it may be just worth while to suggest a possible explanation. It is as follows. These creeping things were a very minor fact in the scheme of creation; so that the purpose of the relator, and the comparative importance of the facts may here, as elsewhere, govern his mode of handling them. It is fit to be observed that he never men-

* "Creation," p. 120.

tions insects at all, as if they were too insignificant to find a place among the larger items of his account; as if he advisedly selected his materials, and sifted off the less important among them. And there does seem to be some license or looseness in his method of treating these creeping things; for while he severs them from fish, fowl, and beast, in the verses I have named, and again in verse 30 from fowl and from beast, yet in verse 28, when the great charter of dominion is granted to man, he sums up in three divisions only, and makes man the lord "over the fish of the sea, and over the fowl of the air, and over every living thing that moveth upon the earth." Reptiles appear to have passed out of his view, either wholly, or so far as not to deserve separate mention, and it may seem likely that he did not think their importance such as to call for a particular and defined place, and, while according to them incidental mention, did not mean to give them such a place, in the chronological order of creation. Let the Contradictionist make the most he can out of this secondary matter: it will not greatly avail.

If, on the whole, such be a fair statement of arguments and results, we may justly render our thanks to Dana, Guyot,* Daw-

---

* In the preface to Guyot's "Creation" will be found some account of the recent literature of this subject. I

son, Stokes, and other scientific authorities, who seem to find no cause for supporting the broad theory of contradiction. I am well aware of my inability to add an atom of weight to their judgments. Yet I have ventured to attempt applying to this great case what I hold to be the just laws of a narrative intended to instruct and to persuade, and thus finding a key to the true construction of the Chapter. For myself, I cannot but at present remain before and above all things impressed with the profound and marvellous wisdom, that has guided the human instrument, whether it were pen or tongue, which was first commissioned from on high, to hand onwards for our admiration and instruction this wonderful, this unparalleled relation. If I am a "reconciler," I shall not call myself a mere apologist, for I aim at a positive, not merely a defensive result, and claim that my reader should feel how true it is that in this brief relation he possesses an inestimable treasure. And I submit to those, who may have closely followed my remarks, that my words

must also mention a valuable pamphlet entitled "The Higher Criticism," by Mr. Rust, Rector of Westerfield, Suffolk. It sets forth the scope of the negative criticism at large, and recommends (p. 30) to "have patience for a while, and wait to see the issue." Similar advice has, I understand, been given in the recent Charge of the learned Bishop of Oxford.

were not wholly idle words, when, without presuming to lay down any universal and inflexible proposition, and without questioning any single contention of persons specially qualified, I said that the true question was whether the words of the Mosaic writer, in his opening chapter, taken as a whole, do not stand, according to our present knowledge, in such a relation to the facts of nature as to warrant and require, thus far, the conclusion that the Ordainer of Nature, and the Giver or Guide of the Creation Story, are One and the Same.

Postscript to the Creation Story.

[Mankind have travelled not by one but by several roads into polytheism. It took a thousand years from the institution of the Mosaic legislation to place the chosen people in a state of security from this insidious mischief. But all along a powerful apparatus of means had been at work, which was strengthened from time to time as Divine Providence saw fit. The foundation, however, had been laid in the Creation Story. It was impossible for those who received it either to travel or to glide into polytheism by either of the widest roads then open, the system of Nature-worship, and the deification of heroes. No one could make the Sun his God, who really believed that there was a God who created the Sun. Even more perhaps was it needful that the line should be clearly and sharply drawn between Deity and humanity, and that a barrier not capable of being surmounted should exclude kings and heroes from deification. In the Homeric or Olympian system, the worship of inanimate nature was studiously shut out; but the beginnings of deification are visible in the case of Heracles,* whose very self (αυτὸς) sits at the banquets of the Immortals, and of the twin brothers, Castor and Pollux, who live and die on alternate days, and who, when they live, receive honors like the gods. In the height of their civilization the Romans set up their living Emperors as divinities. But neither they nor the Greeks believed in the creation of man by the Almighty. The old cosmogonies of the heathen placed matter and other impersonal entities in a position of priority to their gods, who merely take their turn to come upon the scene. Only (I believe) in the Hebrew story is the Deity anterior, without which condition He cannot be supreme.

Besides being anterior, He is separate.

* Od. xi. 302-5.

Did we find in the pages of the Old Testament a story of deification, we should at once know it to be spurious, because in contradiction, alike as to letter and as to spirit, of the entire context.

It is, I hope, not presumptuous to proceed a step further and to say that this broad and effectual severance was necessary not only for the Old dispensation, but for the New: not only for the exclusion of idolatry in all its forms, but for the establishment of the Incarnation. A marriage would be no marriage, unless the individuality of the parties to it were determinate and ineffaceable. The Christian dogma of the two natures in one Person would be in no sense distinctive, if it had been habitual in the preparatory dispensation, as in some of the religions outside it, for man properly so-called to pass into proper deity. Reunion was to be effected between the Almighty and His prime earthly creature by the bridge to be constructed over that flood, the flood of sin, which parted them; and, to sustain that bridge, it was needful that the natures to be brought into union should stand apart like piers perfectly defined, each on its own separate and solid foundation. And the firm foundations of those piers were laid, to endure throughout all time, **by the great Creation Story.**]

The Office and Work of the Old Testament in Outline.

The Office and Work of the Old Testament in Outline.

WE may often hear it said, that the Old Testament is an introduction to the New. Much more is contained in these words, than an irreflective recital may permit us to grasp. Yet they do not seem to cover the whole ground. It seems necessary to glance first at the conjoint function of the two Testaments, in order to measure fully the exalted mission of the earlier. As the heavens cover the earth from east to west, so the Scripture covers and comprehends the whole field of the destiny of man. The whole field is possessed by its moral and potential energy, as a provision enduring to the end of time. But it is marvellous to consider how large a portion of it lies directly within the domain of the Old Testament. The interval to be bridged over between the prophet Malachi and the Advent is not one of such breadth as wholly to abolish a continuity, which was also upheld by visible institutions divinely ordained, and by the production of certain of the Psalms themselves. It is further narrowed in so far as something of a divine *afflatus* is to be found in the books which form the Apocrypha, which are esteemed by a large division of Christendom to be actually a part of the Sacred Canon, and which in the Church of England have a place of special, though secondary, honor. At the more remote end of the scale, it is difficult to name a date for the beginning of the Sacred Scriptures. The corroborative legends of Assyria,* ascertained by modern research, concerning the Creation and the Flood, to which we know not what further additions may still progressively be made, carry us up,† it may be roughly said,

"To the *first* syllable of recorded time."

Historic evidence does not at present warrant our carrying backwards the probable existence of the Adamic race for more than some such epoch as from 4000 to 6000 years before the Advent of Christ. And if, as appears likely, the Creation Story has come down from the beginning, and the Flood legend is also contemporary, the

* These legends will be separately noticed later in the present series of essays.

† See No. VI. of this series for the ground of the argument, which, as here presented, can only have in a certain measure the character of an assumption.

Christian may feel a lively interest in observing that, during by far the larger portion of human history, the refreshing rain of Divine inspiration has descended, with comparatively short intervals, from heaven upon earth, and the records of it have been collected and transmitted in the Sacred Volume. Apart from every question of literary form and detail, we now trace the probable origins of our Sacred Books far back beyond Moses and his time. And so we have a marvellous picture presented to us, not only all-prevailing for the imagination, the heart, and the conscience, of man, but also, as I suppose, quite unexampled in its historical appeal to the human intelligence. The whole human record is covered and bound together in that same unwearied and inviolable continuity, which weaves into a tissue the six Mosaic days of gradually developed creation, and fastens them on at the hither end to the gradually advancing stages of Adamic, and in due course, of subsequent history.

We find then that, apart from the question of moral purity and elevation, the Scriptures of the Old Testament appear to be distinguished from the sacred books possessed by various nations in several vital particulars. They deal with the Adamic race as a whole. They begin with the preparation of the earth for the habitation and use of man. They then, from his first origin, draw downwards a thread of properly personal history, with notices, most remarkable in their character, but contracted in space, of divergent families of men. This thread is enlarged into a web, as from being personal the narrative becomes national, from the Exodus onwards; and eventually it includes the whole race of man. Our Scriptures are not given once for all, as by Confucius or Zoroaster in their respective spheres. They do not deliver a mere code of morals or of legislation, but their character is pre-eminently historical, while they purport to disclose a close and continuing superintendence from on High over human affairs. And the whole is doubly woven into one formation. First, by a chain of Divine action, and of human instructors acting under Divine authority, which is sustained and represented by national institutions, and is never broken until the time when political servitude, like another Egyptian captivity, has become the appointed destiny of the nation. Secondly, by the Messianic bond, by the light of prophecy shining in a dark place, and directing onwards the minds of devout men to the "fulness of time" and the birth of the wondrous Child, so as effectually to link the older sacred books to the dispensation of the Advent, and to carry forward their office through an action both of and in the Church, until the final day of doom. May it not boldly be asked, what parallel to such an outline as this can be supplied by any of the sacred books preserved among any other of the races of the world? So far, then, the office and work of the Old Testament, as presented to us by its own contents, is without a compeer among the old religions. It deals with the case of man as a whole. It covers all time. It is alike adapted to every race and region of the earth. And how, according to the purport of the Old Testament, may that case best be summed up? In these words: it is a history first of sin, and next of redemption.

Our Lord has emphatically said, "They that be whole need not a physician, but they that are sick;"* and this saying goes to the root of the whole matter. Is there or is there not a deep disease in the world, which overflows it like a deluge, and submerges in a great degree the fruit-bearing capacities of our nature? Are we as a race whole, or are we sick, and profoundly sick?

I think that to an impartial eye, and to a thoughtful mind, it must seem strange that there should be a doubt as to the answer to

* Matthew ix. 12.

be given to this question. It seems more easy to comprehend the mental action of those whom the picture of the actual world, as it is unrolled before them, tempts, by its misery, guilt, and shame, into doubt of the being of God, than of persons who can view that picture, and who cannot but observe the dominant part borne by man in determining its character, and yet can make it a subject of question whether man is morally diseased. Veils may have been cast between our vision and the truth of the case by the relative excellence of some select human spirits; by the infinitely varied degrees and forms of the universal malady; by the exaggerations and the narrownesses of outlying schools of theology; and lastly by the remarkable circumstance, that races, above all the extraordinarily gifted race of the ancient Greeks, have lived on into large developments of art, of intellect, and of material power, without creating or retaining any strong conception of moral evil, under the only aspect which reveals its deeper features; that aspect, namely, which presents it to the mind as a departure from the supreme and perfect standard, the will of God. But these disguises are pierced through and through by ever so little of calm reflection. We can conceive how generations, blinded by long abuse to the character of moral evil, could well contrive to blink and pass by the question. But we, who inherit the Christian tradition, ethical as well as dogmatic, cannot, I think, deny the prevalence, perhaps not even the preponderance, of moral evil in the world, without some subtle and preliminary process of degeneracy in our own habit of mind. We shall find that, in renouncing that tradition, we return to a conception which admitted to be evil only that, which was so violently in conflict with the comfort of human society as to require condemnation and repression by its self-preserving laws. The gap between these two conceptions, the one of disordered nature, the other of Divine grace, is immeasurable.

And I think it will not be denied that, in describing vividly the fact of sin in the world, the Scriptures of the Old Testament proceed upon lines, which have also been clearly drawn in the general consciousness at least of the Christian ages. This sense of sin, which lies like a black pall over the entire face of humanity, has been all along the point of departure for every preacher, writer, and thinker within the Hebrew or the Christian fold; and it is the gradual and palpable decline of it, in the literature and society of to-day, that is the darkest among all the signs now overshadowing what is in some respects the bright and hopeful promise of the future.

Nor can any one, who believes in the existence of God, wonder that sin is described as a deviation from the order of nature, as a foreign element, not belonging to the original creation of Divine design, but introduced into it by special causes. At this point we come to what is known as the fall of man, and to the narration of that fall as it is given in the Book of Genesis.

Against this narration the negative criticism has been actively employed. The action ascribed to the serpent is declared to be incredible; the punishment of Adam, disproportioned to the offence, which consisted only in an action not essentially immoral; the punishment of all mankind, for the fault of one, intolerably unjust.

Now let us set entirely aside, for the moment, the form of this narrative, and consider only its substance. Let us deal with it as if it were a parable; in which the severance between the form and the substance is acknowledged and familiar. In proposing this, I do not mean to make on my own part any definitive surrender of the form as it stands, or any admission adverse to it. There is, it may be, high and early Christian authority even for surrendering the form. I only seek to pass within it, and to put the meaning and substance of it upon their trial.

In this relation, we find a certain aggregate of objects, which we are now to treat as if they were simply significant figures. There are presented to us the man, with the woman, in a garden; the serpent, with its faculty of speech; the two trees, of knowledge and of life respectively; a fruit forbidden by Divine command, but eaten in defiance of it; and, after certain reproofs and intimations, ejectment from the garden in consequence. In this ejectment is involved a great deterioration of outward state. But it is not a matter of outward state alone. A deterioration of inward nature is also exhibited, in the derangement of its functions. A new sense of shame bears witness to the revolt * of its lower against its higher elements; and, for the first time, exhibits it to us as a disordered, and therefore a dishonored thing. Together with all this, there is the outline of a promise that, from among the progeny of the fallen pair a Deliverer,

* See Delitzsch, who, in accordance with patristic authorities, writes as follows: "The first consequence of the fall was shame. The nakedness of mankind is no longer the appearance of their innocence. Their corporeity has fallen from the dominion of the spirit. Their beholding has become a sensuous imagining, and the flesh excites their fleshly passions" ("Old Testament History of Redemption," p. 23. Edinburgh: Clark. 1881).

born of woman, shall arise, who, at the cost of personal suffering, shall strike at the very seat of life in the living emblem of evil, and so shall destroy its power. In this relation, on the one hand, many modern objectors have discovered an intolerable folly, and, on the other, the Christian tradition of eighteen centuries has acknowledged a profound philosophy, and a painful and faithful delineation of an indisputable truth.

Now what is the substance conveyed under this form? The Almighty has brought into existence a pair of human beings. He has laid upon them a law of obedience, not to a Decalogue or code, setting forth things essentially good, and the reverse of them, but simply to a rule of feeding and not feeding. The point, at which this representation first brings into view an independent or objective law, lies in the prohibition to feed upon a tree which imparts the knowledge of good and evil. That is to say, the pair, as they then were, were forbidden to aspire to the possession of that knowledge. It was a dispensation of pure obedience.

The question whether this was reasonable or unreasonable cannot be answered upon abstract grounds, but resolves itself into another question, whether it was appropriate or inappropriate to the state of the beings thus addressed, and to their relation towards Him who gave the command. Some may assume that Adam was what so great a writer as Milton has represented him to be—

"For contemplation he and valor formed,"*

and not for contemplation only, but for intricate inquiry and debate on subjects such as tax all the powers of a cultivated intellect. And indeed, if we take the developed man, such as we know him in Christian and civilized society, it seems plain that to lay down for him a law of life which did not include the consideration of essential good and evil, would not only stunt and starve his faculties, but would shock his moral sense.

It may be said that a single act of disobedience, even after full warning, could not so deprave a character as reasonably to entail upon the offender a total change of condition. But I would observe that the school of critics which is apt to take this objection is the very school which, utterly rejecting the literal form of the narrative, is bound to look at it as parable. When so contemplated, its lesson is that rebellion, deliberate and wilful (and this is nothing less),

* "Paradise Lost" (iv. 297).

against just and sovereign authority, fundamentally changes for the worse the character of the rebel. It places him in a new category of motive and action, in which the repetition of the temptation ordinarily begets the repetition of the sin; and it is mercy, not cruelty, which meets this deterioration of character, not with a final and judicial abandonment, but with a deterioration and reduction of state, such as to teach the lesson of retribution, and to serve as an emphatic warning against further sin.

Scripture will lie before us in a true perspective when we come to understand that everywhere the will of God is in accord with the righteousness of God, and that what is promised or inflicted by command is also promised or inflicted by self-acting consequence, according to the constitution of the nature we have received. Religion and philosophy thus join hands, and never part them. When, therefore, we are told that Adam after his sin was shut out from Eden, we are not entitled to say, how hard that he could not be allowed to return, and then perhaps to amend. What is inflicted as penalty from without is acted and suffered in character within. Repentance is not innocence; there must be a remedial process; and, until that process has been faithfully accomplished, the anterior state and habit of mind cannot be resumed.

I do not argue with those who say this is a bad constitution of things, under which sin engenders sinfulness; some better one might surely have been devised. This is to say, "had I been in the Creator's place, I would have managed the business of creation better." It is for us not merely as Christians, but as men of sense, to eschew speculations which even their authors must see to be wholly devoid of practical effect, and to assume the great moral laws and constitution of our nature as ultimate facts, as boundaries which it is futile to attempt to overstep.

To my mind, then, the narrative of the Fall is in accordance with the laws of a grand and comprehensive philosophy, and the objections taken to it are the product of narrower and shallower modes of thought. Introducing us to Adamic man in his first stage of existence—a stage not of savagery but of childhood—it exhibits to us the gigantic drama of his evolution in its opening. In the Paradise of the Book of Genesis, it reduces to a practical form the noble legend of the Golden Age, cherished especially in prehistoric Greece. It wisely teaches us to look to misused free-will as the source of all the sin, and mainly of the accompanying misery, which still overflow the world, and environ human life like a moral deluge. It shows us man in his childhood, no less responsible for disobedience to simple command, than man in his manhood for contravention of those laws of essential right and wrong, which remain now and for ever clothed with the majesty of Divine command. It teaches us how sin begets sin; how the rebellion of the creature against the Creator was at once followed by the rebellion of the creature's lower appetites against his higher mind and will. It impresses upon us that sin is not like the bird lightly flying past us in the air, which closes on it as it goes, and carries no trace behind it. It alters for the worse the very being of the man that acts it, and leaves to him a deteriorated essence. This he in turn, by the inexorable laws of his constitution, transmits to his descendants; and this again in them exhibits, variably, yet on the whole with clear and even glaring demonstration, the evil bias, which it has received; and which it retains until it shall be happily corrected and renewed by those remedial means, which it was the office of the Old Testament to foreshadow, and of the New to establish. Everywhere, then, in this narrative we find that it is instinct with the highest principles of the moral and judicial order.

For the present I pass by the Flood*
and the Dispersion,† which may be most
conveniently considered in connection with
what is termed profane history; and I touch
next upon the call of Abraham. This call
imports the selection of a peculiar and
separate family, which was afterwards to
grow into a people. They were to be in a
special degree the subjects of God's care,
the guardians of His Word, and the vehicles
of His promises. Of all great and distinctive chapters in the Biblical history of the
human race since Paradise, we have here
perhaps the greatest and the most distinctive.

The selection of a family may be regarded
from many points of view.

When sin had come into the world, it developed itself in the forms of infirmity, and of
apostasy: if it be allowed to describe rudely
by their general terms the form of character
which distinguished the race of Cain from the
race of Seth. What we see of the former is, as
described in Gen. iv. 16-24, its rapid advance,
and apparently its marked precedence, in
arts and powers. It disappears entirely
with the story of the Flood; and we are
left to infer that it may have had a principal
share in calling down that great retribution
inflicted upon revolt from God.

After the Deluge, in the time of Peleg,

* Genesis vi.–viii. † Genesis x.

fifth from Noah, selection again appears, and is carried down in Gen. xi. to Abraham, from whom an unbroken thread runs onward into the period when the chosen family had become a chosen nation.

This choice of a particular family or race may be advantageously contrasted with the heathen method of selection or preference, by the deification of individuals. Of the first, it is obvious that it reached over all time; that in this way it tended to assert the unity of the human race; and that it was never exclusive, as it always (not to mention other proofs) invited to partake of its benefits the "stranger" with whom it had come into contact. The rival method of deification broke communion rather than established it, and was based on no rational principle of choice. It was corrupt as well as arbitrary, for the deified were not the best. But what I would here chiefly press is, that the continuous selection of a family was a bar to deification, because deification was essentially founded on individualities; instead of that headship in series, which presented to humanity as its chiefs a lineage. Of this every member had his destiny as it were locked into that of the rest by an essential parity. This kind of selection did not favor idolatry, like the other, but built up a wall against it. And so it came about, as we have seen, that, even when idolatry invaded and possessed the people, it never tainted the religion.

This selection of Abraham and his progeny, if we speak after the manner of men, we might perhaps describe as follows. The original attempt to plant a species upon our planet, which should be endowed with the faculty of free-will, but should always direct that will to good, had been frustrated through sin; and the tainted progeny had, after a trial of many generations, been destroyed by the Deluge. In the descendants of Noah, man was renewed upon a far larger scale. Different branches of the race* were sent, or were allowed to go forth, and to people different portions of the earth, each carrying with them different gifts, and different vocations according to those gifts; the notes of which, in various prominent cases, we cannot fail to discern written large upon the page of history. After a brief period, choice was made not of a nation, but of a person, namely, Abraham, who with his descendants became the subject of a special training. They lived, according to the record in the Bible, not like other men generally, dependent upon the exercise of their natural faculties alone, but with the advantage from time to time,

* Genesis x.

and with the continuing responsibility, of supernatural command and visitation. But this remarkable promotion to a higher form of life did not invest them with any arbitrary or selfish prerogative. On the contrary, as the legislation of Moses was distinguished from other ancient codes by its liberal and likewise elaborate care for the stranger; so also, from the very outset, and before the family could blossom into the nation, nay, even in the very person of Abraham, the gift imparted to him was declared to be given for the behoof of mankind at large. "In thee and in thy seed shall all the families of the earth be blessed."* The prerogative of the Jew was, from its very inception, bound up with the future elevation of the Gentile.

This divine election doubtless carried with it the duty and the means of reaching a higher level of moral life than prevailed among the surrounding Asiatic nations. These nations, sharing with the chosen race the infirmity and deterioration of nature, differed in this, that they at once carried the reflection of their own sinfulness into their creed respecting the unseen, and made religion itself a direct instrument of corruption. Yet those, whom we call the patriarchs, were not exempted from the general

* Genesis xxviii. 14.

degeneracy of morals; and even Abraham, the general strain of whose life appears to have been so simple and devout, on going down into Egypt to escape from famine, exposed his wife to the risk of an adulterous connection with the king of the country, lest, if she were known to be his wife, his personal safety should be compromised. On the moral standing of the nation sprung from Abraham, as compared with that of contemporary races, there will be more to say hereafter. Meantime, it may be observed that the sins and follies of the favored race, as well as of their priests and rulers, are told in the narrative frankly, and without attempting to excuse them. This frankness of narration extends also to the calamities which befell the Israelites; and, as an evidence of the integrity of the Hebrew penmen, it suggests a presumption that such plain speaking, in the face of national and ancestral self-love, is, to say the least, highly in accordance with the belief that the record generally was framed under special guidance from above.

The selection of Abraham and his posterity was at the least a boon to some, a privation to none. In its immediate effect, it withdrew nothing from the nations outside the Hebrew pale. It bestowed, indeed, upon the parallel line of Ishmael a preferential but inferior blessing, which, however, it is no part of the present purpose to examine, further than to say that the Mohammedan religion may be regarded, in its conflict with the idolatry which it first confronted, and in the present day among the tribes of Western Africa, as having been, if not permanently yet for a time, the communication of a relative good. And the Old Testament abounds with passages which demonstrate the care, and even the special care, of the Almighty for nations other than the Jews.*

But the object, which now demands our attention, is the promise of a blessing in and by the seed of Abraham to all the nations of the earth. The first-fruits of this blessing may be said to have been perceived in the translation of the books of the Old Testament into Greek during the third century before the Advent. At the time when the language of the Greeks was maturing its supremacy, in the East through the conquests of Alexander the Great, and in the West through appreciation by the Roman and Italian genius, in some respects allied to their own, the Greek race itself was on its decline, both as to its intellect and as to its practical energy. This decline may, per-

* See, for example, the two first chapters of Amos, and the whole book of Jonah.

haps, have rendered the world more receptive of the influences, which the substance of the Hebrew books was calculated to exercise.

There can hardly be a doubt that, among all the forms of Hellenic thought exhibited in the different schools of philosophy, that of the Stoics was the highest in respect of its conception of the Deity, of its emancipation from idolatry, and of its capacity of moral elevation. In the hands of Seneca, of Epictetus, and of Marcus Aurelius, Stoic ideas attained so high a level as to have been used by some in disparagement of the exclusive claim of the Gospel to the promulgation of truths powerful enough to regenerate the world. Without asserting that the early Stoics derived their inspiration through the Greek version, called the Septuagint, from the Hebrew Scriptures, it may be observed that, as a matter of fact, philosophy rose to its highest level through the Stoics at a time when the Greek mind was declining; and further, that Stoicism made its first appearance, and began its advance, at the epoch when those Scriptures had become accessible. Also it arose and flourished not in Greece itself, but at points such as Citium, in countries such as Pontus, in schools of learning such as Alexandria, which were seats of Jewish resort and influence.*

It was an advance of a different order towards the fulfilment of the Abrahamic promises, when the Apostles, charged with the commission of our Lord, went forth into all the world, and preached the gospel to every creature.† Then, indeed, an enginery was set at work, capable of coping with the whole range of the mischiefs brought into the world by sin, and of completely redeeming the human being from its effects, and consecrating our nature to duty and to God. It is impossible here to do so much as even to skirt this vast subject. But at once these three things may be said as to the development, through the Gospel, of the Abrahamic promise. First, that in the vast aggregate of genuine believers, the recovery of the Divine image has been effectual, and the mainspring of their being has been set right before their

* See "Encycl. Britann." 9th ed. Art. Stoics. It states that "the school is mainly to be considered as the first-fruits of that interaction between West and East, which followed the conquests of Alexander. Zeno was of Phœnician descent; Cyprus, Silicia, Syria, the main countries of its origin. Citium, Alexandria, Heraclea, Pontus, were prominent among the places furnishing and rearing its teachers. Most of the Stoics were from lands of Hellenistic (as distinct from Hellenic) civilization. It was the growth of the Hellenized East."

† Mark xvi. 15.

quitting the world, by the dedication of the will to God. Secondly, that the social results of the change have been beneficial and immense, in the restriction of wars, in the abolition of horrible practices publicly sanctioned; in the recognition of essential rights; in the elevation of woman (whose case most and best of all represents the case of right as against force); in the mitigation of selfish and cruel laws; in the refinement of manners; in the utter proscription of all extreme forms of sin; and in the public acknowledgment of standards of action nearer to the true. Thirdly, that Christendom is at this moment undeniably the prime and central power of the world, and still bears, written upon its front, the mission to subdue it. In point of force and onward impulsion, it stands without a rival, while every other widely spread religion is in decline. Critical, indeed, are the movements which affect it from within. Vast are the deductions which on every side are to be made from the fulness of the Divine promises, when we try to measure their results in the world of facts. Indefinitely slow, and hard to trace in detail, as may be, like a glacier in descent, the march of the times, the Christianity of to-day has, in relation to the world non-Christian, an amount of ascendency such as it has never before possessed; and, if only it can sufficiently retain its inward consistency, the sole remaining question seems to be as to the time, the circumstances, and the rate of its further, perhaps of its final, conquests.

I know that it is far beyond the scope of a few pages such as these to make good in detail the claims of the Abrahamic promise. Still, I think that even what has been said may in some measure suffice for the purpose which I have immediately in view. That purpose is to establish in outline the strictly exceptional character of the books of the Old Testament; and with this aim to show that they bear upon them the stamp of a comprehensiveness which concerns, which penetrates, nay, which envelops the history of the world as a whole. The promise, given to Abraham nearly two thousand years before the Advent, finds its correlative marks in the general train of subsequent history. These marks demonstrate that it was given by a Divine foreknowledge. And if so, then the venerable record in which it is enshrined surely seems here, at least, to carry the seal and signature of a Divine authorship.

Now let us consider from another point of view the selection of the Hebrew race, and the peculiar standing of the Mosaic legislation, so intimately allied with the whole of its singularly chequered fortunes. And in order to effect something towards ascertaining what was probably the cause determining the Divine selection and procedure, we may do well first to refer to some aims which might at first sight have been thought probable; such as, to provide a complete theology; or such as, to reward with honor, wealth, and power a peculiarly virtuous people, whose moral conduct was to be of a nature likely to make them an edifying and attractive example to the nations of the earth. Human speculation might have been forward to anticipate that one or both of these aims might have been contemplated by a plan so exceptional, as the selection and isolation of one particular line and people. But the facts appear to show that any such anticipation would have been entirely mistaken.

By a complete theology, I mean simply such a theology as would confront and make provision for all the leading facts of the moral situation. Among these a prominent place had from the date of the first traditions been given to the entrance of sin into the world, and to the promise of redemption from its power. Now it is evident that there was no attempt, in the legislation of the Pentateuch, at this theological completeness. Its theology is summed up in clear declarations of the being of God and of duty and love to Him, with which are directly associated, in the Decalogue, the main items of man's duty to his neighbor, and, both there and elsewhere, the doctrines of rewards and punishments. The race also inherited the narrative of what is termed in Christian theology the Fall of Man. This, however, was part of the anterior tradition; and, though implied in the Mosaic system, was neither directly set forth in its terms, nor made a common subject of allusion in the historic books, however it may have been involved in the sacrificial system.

But these rewards and punishments are of a temporal nature; and the Mosaic legislation is thought to give no indication of a future state or of an Underworld. This is the more remarkable, because the early chapters of Genesis, although they usually contain but the merest outline of history, are not without such indication.* Enoch, at the end of his 365 years, "was not, for God took him." These remarkable words are substituted for the formula given in the cases of the other patriarchs, whose record closes with the phrase, "and he died."† Here there seems to be a clear manifestation of the state into which Enoch is de-

* Genesis v. 24.   † *Ibid.* v. 5, and *passim.*

clared to have entered, without passing through the gate of death.

Again, we now know, from the Egyptian Book of the Dead and otherwise, that the religious system of that country not only included, but was greatly based upon, the conception of a future life. It seems absolutely impossible that the Israelites, even had they not been aware of it already, could have dwelt for many generations in the land of Egypt without coming to know of it. Our Lord Himself affirms that they knew it in His time.* And we have it exhibited to us in the Psalms,† which exhibit the interior and spiritual life of chosen souls.

It has, perhaps, been too much the practice to assume that the Mosaic law is to be regarded as an enlargement of the patriarchal religion. Without doubt it is at least a very large and important supplement to that religion. But a supplement differs from an enlarged and reconstructed edition: it is less, as well as more. It need not contain everything contained in that to which it is a supplement. Here is a great and vital particular, in which the Mosaic law cannot be said even to have republished the patriarchal religion; and which both

---

* Matthew xxii. 32; Mark xii. 27.
† For example, Psalms xvi. 10; xlix. 15.

preceded and survived the law, but did not find a place in it. Accordingly, among the Jews of the Advent, the school which most rigidly adhered to the letter of the law, namely, that of the Sadducees,* denied the future state, and held "that there is no resurrection, neither angel nor spirit."

We are not, therefore, to suppose that Israel was without the hope of a future life, which St. Peter on the Day of Pentecost himself demonstrated out of the Sixteenth Psalm;† but only to perceive that the Mosaic legislation was limited to its proper purpose; that, namely, of setting apart a nation from the rest of mankind, and providing it with peculiar means and guarantees for the fulfilment of its mission as a nation. It erected a walled precinct, within which the ancient belief of the fathers was to find shelter and to thrive, while it was wofully dwindling and perishing among all the kindred nations of the world. It supplied an impregnable home for personal religion. But personal religion, taken by itself, is conspicuously weak in the means of transmission from age to age. The sons of Eli were wicked persons, and the evil Manasseh succeeds the pious Hezekiah. It is not without the aid of fixed and solid institutions, which take hold upon masses of

* Acts xxiii. 8.   † Acts ii. 25.

men collectively, that the sacred fire is kept alive among us. Hence our Lord did not merely teach His holy precepts, and fulfil His Divine career in His own person, but founded His Church on earth, to carry His work onwards even to the day of doom. And hence, under the guidance of the Most High, Moses was commissioned to establish a system which, without being in itself complete, provided for the double purpose, first, of building up a fortress (so to call it) within whose wall true spiritual religion might in singular fulness flourish and abound; and, secondly, of establishing a firmly knit national system of doctrine and worship, intended to secure the permanent purity of belief in the one self-existent God, and the continuing practice of a ritual which set forth in act the existence of sin, and made intelligible and familiar to the people at large some need of deliverance from it by reconciliation. And so, through the long ages from the Exodus to the Advent, there lived on the two systems together, distinct but accordant. The one was the religion of interior devotion, powerfully upheld and stimulated, as occasion offered, by the Prophets, and continually exercised and developed in the public ritual by the Psalms. The other was the religion of exterior worship. This was full of significance. It had a command over the entire people. It was incorporated in public laws and institutions, and was associated at every point with the national life. These outer means so operated as to exempt the higher and interior treasure from the risks of dependence on short-lived individual fervor, and provided secure means for its transmission from age to age.

We have in the institution of the prophetic school the setting forth of a profound lesson, which reminds us that the Mosaic system was alike in itself necessary, and of itself insufficient.

From another, and possibly even more commanding, point of view, we perceive the insufficiency of Mosaism to fill up fully the outlines of the Divine dispensations. Sin, in the form of disobedience to Divine command, had entered into the world, and had utterly marred the fair order which, at the outset, the Almighty had noted in His Creation. The mischief was not left to stand alone; and the promise of a Redeemer from it was immediately delivered. Thus far, the Mosaic system helps us; yet, in helping us, tells us to look beyond itself. By its system of sacrifice it threw into distinct relief the idea that offence had been committed, and that our standing was not upright before God. Now with this were associated in Genesis the further ideas that from this offence there would be a way of reconciliation and recovery, and that this way would be found in a member of the human race, a portion of the seed of the woman. On these further ideas Mosaism so far threw light, that it pointed through sacrifice to pardon; but it added nothing of force or clearness to the original promise that this recovery should be wrought out in and through a Redeemer having the form and the nature of man. This prophecy of the Incarnation, though a vital portion of the ancient tradition of the patriarchs, did not derive any supplement or new enforcement from the construction of the Hebrew laws and institutions. It remained, and it propagated itself, mainly in the Psalms and in the Prophets, while its root was pre-Mosaic. Some rays of the light of that promise may perhaps be traced, outside the Hebrew precinct, in particular traditions of the heathen world. There may be vestiges of it in that close vital association between Deity and humanity, which marked the Greek or Olympian religion; but which, as the fundamental conception of sin more and more faded away, lost all its moral force. Mosaism did essential and infinite service in deeply sculpturing (so to speak) the idea of sin in the human consciousness; but it was not favorable to that theanthropy, or union of the Divine and human, of which the human side had been so strongly foreshadowed in the original charter. Perhaps by the rigid prohibition of images, which was so necessary for its direct purpose, it rather tended to widen the distance, at which man stood as a being worshipping his Maker. Already idolatry, such as prevailed in the East, was associated with the human form, and the necessity of shutting out that idolatry may have carried with it, in this respect, a certain religious incompleteness as a consequence.

I now come to the second supposition; and I ask whether the selection of the Hebrew race was grounded on their moral superiority. Within narrow limits, the answer would be affirmative. They were appointed to purge and to possess the land of Canaan on account of the terrible and loathsome iniquities of its inhabitants. The nations whom they were to subdue had reached that latest stage of sensual iniquity, which respects neither God nor nature. The sensual power within man, which rebelled against him when he had rebelled against God, had in Canaan enthroned its lawlessness as law, and its bestial indulgences had become recognized, normal, nay more, even religious and obligatory. And there are those in the present day who, admitting the facts, find in them a subject of pleasurable contemplation, as if they simply exhibited an innocent and free exercise of natural propensities. The propensities were due indeed to nature; but only to nature in a condition of disorder and disease.

The vicious practices of these nations, indicated rather than described in the Old Testament, and veiled, apparently for decency's sake, in the translations, are too sadly attested by the character of the remains, which, in later times, archæology has recovered from their hiding-places. They are also attested by the poems of Homer. In these poems, the Phœnicians represent Syrian religion, and we find the goddess Aphroditè, whose debased worship it seems plain that they were gradually importing into Greece, to have stood for little more than a symbol of lawless lust. This is "Ashtoreth, the goddess of the Zidonians." *

I find it much more difficult to answer the question, whether the Hebrew race were planted in the land of promise, which flowed with milk and honey, by reason of, or in connection with, their moral superiority to the nations of the world taken universally. It is, down to the present day, extremely

* 1 Kings xi. 5–33.

difficult to make any trustworthy estimate of the comparative moral standing even of any two contemporary peoples. It may be admitted that the form of human nature has with the modern conditions grown far more manifold and complex. But, on the other hand, in answering the question I have just put, we have the difficulty not only of remoteness in time, but of extreme scantiness of information.

I shall assume that the mass of the children of Israel at large were trained mainly by Mosaism, and little in comparison by the more highly spiritual tradition conserved and enshrined within it. Speaking of these, we may consider that the Old Testament gives us more than a sketch, if less than a picture, of their social and moral state. I am aware of only one other race, with respect to which we have any account possessing a tolerable fulness. That is the race of the Achaian Greeks, painted with marvellous force as well as completeness by Homer. The poet describes the manners of one generation; the books of the Old Testament, say from Abraham to the Captivity, range over many. Still, numerous as these are, they present a considerable unity of color. I carefully reserve the case of that inner and elect circle among the Hebrews, to whom we owe the possession down to this day of inestimable spiritual treasures. But comparing, as well as I am able, ordinary or average life among the ordinary Hebrews on the one side, and the ordinary Greeks of Homer (whom I take to have lived long after Moses, but considerably before the age of David) on the other, I cannot discern that these last were in a moral sense inferior.

I am sensible, however, that in such a proposition as has just been uttered there must be, to the general reader, some appearance of paradox; and likewise that such an appearance will not be effectually removed by reference to the Scriptural complaints of the stiff neck, or the hard heart, of the Israelites. I must therefore make further endeavors to get at the truth of the case before us.

I do not feel that even the patriarchal history is designed to convey to us the idea that the privileged race stood uniformly at a great moral elevation, as compared with other and ordinary portions of mankind.

The subject is a painful one, and I shall not dilate upon its details. But it seems undeniable that, in the history of the selected line, we find from time to time the development of wickedness in its extreme forms. Such are the sin of Onan,* the incest of

* Genesis xxxviii. 8, 9.

the daughters of Lot,* and the brutal insensibility of Ham, the son of Noah, to the claims of natural decency.† Nor are the women exempt, as we learn from the incest devised and effected by Tamar.‡ And the wife of Lot cast a yearning look on the hell of Sodom.§ The first three cases, and the last, are not in the line of the ultimate succession; but Pharez, the son of Tamar, is the recorded ancestor of King David and his descendants.‖ Now, among the Achaian Greeks of Homer we find a sensitive delicacy, altogether peculiar, as to all exposure of the person. There is nowhere any extreme form of sensual indulgence. Among the Bœotian immigrants from the East, that is from the Syrian coast, there occurred at an early stage of their history in the Peninsula, a case of incest;¶ but it was always regarded by the indigenous tradition as involuntary, and what is more, a curse clave on this account to the race of Kadmos, and brought about its early extinction.

While incest is thus regarded as a monstrous perversion of nature among the Greeks, there are in the Homeric poems, as I think, sufficiently clear indications that

* Genesis xix. 32. † Genesis ix. 22.
‡ Genesis xxxviii. 6-30. § Genesis xix. 26.
‖ Matthew i. 3-5. ¶ Od. xi. 271-4.

it was practised without shame among the Phœnicians,* the coast-neighbors of Syria, and partners with it in manners, if not also probably in race.

Let us now turn to two others among the great moral constituents of human character, and consider the case of humanity as against cruelty, and of truth as against fraud.

Let us take the two cases first of the deceit practised by Jacob upon his brother Esau and his father Isaac; secondly, of the base and unnatural conduct of the sons of Jacob towards their brother Joseph. As there is nothing recorded in favor of the Homeric or Achaian Greeks which approaches in moral beauty to the forgiveness freely accorded by Joseph, so there is nothing recorded against them which so wickedly tramples down the laws of nature, as the flagrant iniquities to which attention has just been called. The conduct of the suitors of Penelope in the Odyssey, and the actions of Paris (a foreigner), supply the worst exhibitions of human nature which come before us in the Poems. Both there and in the Old Testament retribution follows guilt, but what I now speak of is the depth of guilt, not its treatment. There is nowhere in Homer a case, between relatives, of deceit

*Od. x. 7, and less flagrantly, vii. 64–8.

like that of Jacob, or of cruelty like that of his sons.

When we come to the Palestinian period, it would appear that the Israelites were subjected to a force and diversity of temptations, such as perhaps no people ever had to encounter. Successful war had stimulated their vindictive passions. Triumph everywhere had waited on their arms. They were entitled to esteem themselves the directly chosen ministers of God. They were likely to regard the heathen, among whom they came, with hatred and contempt. They passed from a life, wandering, uncertain and ill supplied, to settlement and to abundance. The temples or emblems of seductive lust everywhere met their eyes; and the vile example, by which they were solicited in the mass and in detail, pretended plausibly to hallow itself by close association with religion. There is scarcely an evil passion that finds entrance into the human breast which was not powerfully stirred by the circumstances of the Israelitish conquest. We find in the sacred text indications of the severity of some of their temptations. Take, for instance, Deut. vi. 10-16; and again in xxxi. 20 it is written,

"For when I shall have brought them into the land which I sware unto their fathers, that floweth with milk and honey; and they shall have eaten and filled themselves, and waxen fat; then will they turn unto other gods and serve them, and provoke me, and break my covenant."

The general indication seems to be first the perpetuation of a chosen seed, at the very heart of the nation, high in the knowledge of interior religion; secondly, a decided ethical superiority of the Hebrew line over the Asiatic nations in their neighborhood, as indeed it was from Asia that the extremes of corruption flowed into the Greek Peninsula in the earliest historic times. Yet the loveliest picture of womanhood in all the early sacred books is that of Ruth; and Ruth was of the children of Moab, who was the incestuous offspring of one of the daughters of Lot.*

Humanity, or mercy, is certainly not the strong point of the Achaian Greeks. With them not only no sacredness, but little value, attached to human life; and the loss of it stirs no sympathy unless it be associated with beauty, valor, patriotism, or other esteemed characteristics. Yet here, again, the forms of evil are less extreme. We do not find, even in the stern, relentless vengeance of Odysseus on his enemies, or in the passionate wish of Achilles that nature would permit what it forbade, namely, to devour his hated foe, a form of cruelty and

* Genesis xix. 36–7.

brutality so savage as is recorded in the case of the Levite with his wife and concubine at Gibeah, and of the war which followed it.*

The temptations of lust were even more formidable, than those of cruelty and revenge. According to the sacred text, this danger was foreseen from the first; and the very earliest Mosaic legislation,† after that of the Commandments, begins to denounce a portion of the indescribable practices which were rife among the older occupiers of the promised land. It was subsequently carried into further particulars, and we know that, down the whole course of the historic period before the Captivity, the filthy idolatry not only encircled the chosen people, but at times so invaded it, as to reduce to a remnant the untainted portion of the community, the true worshippers of God. Even pious monarchs were sometimes afraid to destroy its constituted, and in a perverse sense, consecrated emblems.

On the other hand, we must not view the case of the earliest Greeks in the spirit of optimism. War and its devastations were with them habitual and almost normal; property was little respected; cunning, as well as skill, was sometimes held in honor. Yet it remains a broad and indisputable

* Judges xix.–xxi. † Exodus xxii. 16.

truth that honor and truth, as well as valor, were prevailingly respected, that family ties were very sacred, that the law of nature was simply and profoundly revered, and that the extreme forms of vice and sin, the widest and most hopeless departures from the law of God, are nowhere to be found in any of their forms.

Enough has perhaps been said to show that we cannot claim as a thing demonstrable a great moral superiority for the Hebrew line generally over the whole of the historically known contemporary races. This, however, leaves ample room for the belief that there was an interior circle, known to us by its fruits in the Psalter and the prophetic books, of a morality and sanctity altogether superior to what was to be found elsewhere, and due rather to the pre-Mosaic, than to the Mosaic, religion of the race. But it remains to answer with reverence the question, Why, if not for a distinctly superior morality, nor as a full religious provision for the whole wants of man, *why* was the race chosen, as a race, to receive the promises, to guard the oracles, and eventually, to fulfil the hopes, of the great Redemption?

The answer may, I believe, be conveyed in moderate compass. The design of the Almighty, as we everywhere find, was to prepare the human race, by a varied and a prolonged education, for the arrival of the greatest epoch of history. The immediate purposes of the Abrahamic selection may have been to appoint, for the task of preserving in the world the fundamental bases of religion, a race, which possessed qualifications for that end decisively surpassing those of all other races. We may easily indicate two of these fundamental bases. The first was the belief in one God. The second was the knowledge that mankind at large had departed from His laws; without which knowledge how should they welcome a Deliverer, whose object it was to bring them back? It may be stated with confidence that among the dominant races of the world the belief in one God was speedily destroyed by polytheism, and the idea of sin faded gradually but utterly away. Is it audacious to say that what was wanted was a race so endowed with the qualities of masculine tenacity and persistency, as to hold over in safe custody these all-important truths until that fulness of time, when, by and with them, the complete design of the Almighty would be revealed to the world? A long experience of trials beyond all example has proved since the Advent how the Jews, in this one essential quality, have all along surpassed every other people upon earth. A marvellous and glorious experience has shown how among their ancestors before the Advent were kept alive and in full vigor the doctrine of belief in one God, and the true idea of sin. These our Lord, when He came, found ready to His hand, essential pre-conditions of His teaching. And, in the exhibition of this great and unparalleled result of a most elaborate and peculiar discipline, we may perhaps recognize, sufficiently for the present purpose, something of the Office and Work of the Old Testament.

The Psalms.

The Psalms.

I.—THEIR HISTORIC PLACE IN THE DEVOTION OF ALL AGES.

JOHN BRIGHT has told me that he would be content to stake upon the Book of Psalms, as it stands, the great question whether there is or is not a Divine Revelation. It was not to him conceivable how a work so widely severed from all the known productions of antiquity, and standing upon a level so much higher, could be accounted for except by a special and extraordinary aid calculated to produce special and extraordinary results; for it is reasonable, nay needful, to presume a due correspondence between the cause and the effect. Nor does this opinion appear to be unreasonable. If Bright did not possess the special qualifications of the scholar or the critic, he was, I conceive, a very capable judge of the moral and religious elements in any case that had been brought before him by his personal experience.

It was in truth a noble distinction of the Hebrew race to have produced persons imbued with such qualities and gifts, as were capable of composing the Book of Psalms.

Twice in his Epistles (Eph. v. 19; Col. iii. 16) does St. Paul admonish Christians upon musical services as a fitting vent for the devout mind and heart. In both cases he employs the same phraseology, and enjoins the use of "psalms and hymns and spiritual songs," each time giving the first place in the enumeration to Psalms. I find it difficult to dismiss the idea that in this word the use of the Psalter was either intended or included; especially as there are early testimonies to the effect that antiphonal singing was in use from the origin of the Church.*

Upon the most superficial survey of the Psalms in their general aspect, it seems difficult or impossible to regard them as simply owing their parentage to the Mosaic system. Some, indeed, of their features may well be referred to it; especially the strong sense of national unity which they display, and the concentration of that sense upon a single centre, the city of Jerusalem and the temple.

It may also be noted that the Mosaic law inculcated in its utmost breadth the princi-

* As to the last-named point, see Wordsworth and Alford, *in loco*.

ple of love to God. "Thou shalt love the Lord thy God with all thine heart, and with all thy soul, and with all thy might."* Yet may it not be said, from the place in which it occurs, that this is rather exhortation than statute? Further, it is not unfolded in the detail of the legislative Torah; and, even in the Decalogue, service is enjoined without the mention of love. The early books do not exhibit, like the Psalter, the close, inner contact of the individual soul with the Deity; and, as water does not rise above the source, it is hard to ascribe to them alone the wonderful development of that principle which pervades the body of this unparalleled collection. We seem compelled to assume for them some loftier fountain-head of instruction. This, I would submit, is in part supplied, and in part suggested, by the Book of Genesis. I say suggested, inasmuch as the outlines of a primeval religion drawn in that book are not less slight than they are significant. So slight, indeed, that I have been unable to resist the impression that there were supplementary communications of Divine truth, over and above those contained in Holy Writ, and perhaps traceable, here and there, in later portions of the Old Testament and of the Apocryphal Books. And I also say

* Deut. vi. 4, 5.

supplied, inasmuch as the story of the Fall involves in full the idea of our restoration in character as well as condition, which is nowhere enunciated in the Law; and further, inasmuch as it sets forth, at least down to the time of Abraham, a personal intercourse, habitual and direct, with the Deity, and one pointing onwards to the great Redemption.

In a preceding essay I have represented that the Mosaic law was not the promulgation of a new and complete religion, but a code of provisions intended for the particular purpose (1) of building up a wall of effectual separation between the Jewish community, and the corruption of the nations whose land they were to conquer and to possess; and (2) of preserving in vitality and freshness, within that precinct, the fundamental conceptions of the Divine unity and righteousness, and of the duty and the sinfulness of man. These all-important propositions were the necessary pre-conditions of any plan for the restoration of peace in a disordered world. But they were, nevertheless, in process of extirpation from the general and public religion of all those Gentile races, whose history is given us in Scripture, or in the classical books of profane antiquity.

Thus the Mosaic system, while it was

defensive against the surrounding iniquity, was also something more, and something higher. That system, both institutional and doctrinal, fenced in, as it were, a clear space, a free and secure domain, for the fuller development of a religion, inward and personal, devotional and spiritual, the materials for which it could hardly have supplied by presenting, as it did, God as ruler and judge, and man as a servant who continually either sinned, or was on the brink of falling into sin.

In the inner sanctuary, thus provided for the most capable human souls, was reared the strong spiritual life, which appears to have developed itself pre-eminently in the depth, richness, tenderness, and comprehensiveness of the Psalms. To the work they have here accomplished, there is no parallel upon earth. For the present I put aside all details, and am content to stand upon this fact—that a compilation, which began (at the latest) with a shepherd of Palestine, three thousand years ago, has been the prime and paramount manual of devotion from that day to this; first for the Hebrew race, both in its isolation, and after it was brought, by the translation of its sacred books, into relations with the Gentile world; and then for all the Christian races, in all their diversities of character and circumstance. Further, that there is now, if possible, less chance than ever of the displacement of these marvellous compositions from their supremacy in the worship of the Christian church. And beyond doubt it may be also said that their function has not been one of ritual pomp and outward power alone. They have dwelt in the Christian heart, and at the very centre of that heart; and wherever the pursuits of the inner life have been most largely conceived and cultivated, there, and in the same proportion, the Psalms have towered over every other vehicle of general devotion. We have a conspicuous illustration of their office in the fact that of two hundred and forty-three actual citations from the Old Testament found in the pages of the New, no less than one hundred and sixteen are from the single Book of Psalms; and that a similar proportion holds with most of the early Fathers.* Bishop Alexander has published the result of a careful examination made by himself. It is, that reference is made to the Psalms,

* Canon Cook, in the Speaker's Bible, vol. iv. p. 146. There is a minor, but still not unmeaning, indication to the same effect, which it would be unseemly to couple with that given in the text, but which I venture to name for its recency, and because it is eminently associated with the general course of modern life. In a manual, not of hymns, but of devotions prepared for public use in the mixed congregations on board a great line of packet

either by quotation or otherwise, in no fewer than two hundred and eighty-six passages of the New Testament.*

We have thus before us the fact that the Psalms, composed for the public worship of the Hebrews from two to three thousand years ago, constitute down to the present day for Christians the best and highest book of devotion. A noteworthy fact even on the surface of it; more noteworthy still, when we go below the surface into the meaning. The Hebrews were Semitic, Christendom is (chiefly) Aryan; the Hebrews were local, Christendom is worldwide; the Hebrews were often tributary, and finally lost their liberties and place among the nations; Christianity has mounted over every obstacle, and has long been the dominating power of the world. The Hebrews had no literature outside their religion, nor any Fine Art; Christendom has appropriated, and even rivalled, both the literature and the art of the greatest among the ancients. This strange book of Hebrew devotions had no attraction outside Hebrewism, except for Christians; and Christians

---

ships from Great Britain to North America. I find that, out of 254 pages, 137 are occupied by selections from the Psalms; the chief part of the remainder being a collection of hymns.

* " The Witness of the Psalms." Note A, p. 291.

have found nothing to gather, in the same kind, from any of the other religions in the world. The stamp of continuity and identity has been set upon one, and one only, historic series; one and one only, thread runs down through the whole succession of the ages; and, among many witnesses to this continuity, the Psalms are probably among the most conspicuous. This stamp purports to be, and to have been all along, Divine; and the unparalleled evidence of results all goes to show that it is not a forgery.

The wonderful phenomenon thus presented to us can hardly be said to admit of enhancement; and yet it is, perhaps, enhanced, when we bear in mind that the long period of this perpetual youth, exhibited by the Psalms, has been one broken by the promulgation of a new religion, together with all the changes of fact, and developments of principle, which transformed the heathen world.

Moreover, we should remember that the shapings of all language merely human are essentially shortlived, and forms of speech succeed one another as wave follows upon wave. But herein seems probably to lie one of the ways in which the Divine revelation asserts itself. It appears to have the faculty of giving to things mutable the privilege and the power of the immutable, and to endow fashions of speech, when they belong to the heart's core of human nature, with a charter that is to endure throughout all time.

I submit, then, that the fact of so wonderful a power as was thus exercised by the Psalms, in such diversities of time, race, and circumstances, is not only without parallel, but is removed by such a breadth of space from all other facts of human experience in the same province, as to constitute in itself a strong presumption that the cause also is one lying beyond the range of ordinary human action, and may most reasonably be set down as consisting in that specialty of Divine suggestion and guidance, which we term revelation.

II.—THEIR ANTIQUITY.

The antiquity of the Book of Psalms, like that of the other books of Scripture, does not directly or necessarily involve the essence of the case concerning them, which I apprehend is more dependent upon their character and their results. Yet it counts, for importance, in the next order of considerations, since the form and substance are here more intimately allied than in the terms used for the recital of events in an historical book.

It is also to be assumed that the incessant use of the Psalms in the service of the temple, and the comparatively wide knowledge of them thus conveyed to the people, were in the nature of special securities for their faithful and exact transmission.

When we speak of the Psalms of David, we use a popular and general form of expression, which names the whole from the largest or most weighty, and, originally, most conspicuous, of the parts. The phrase is sufficiently shown not to be absolute and precise by the beautiful 137th Psalm, which describes the condition of the Hebrews in Babylon, five centuries after the death of the minstrel King. Seventy-three Psalms* in all are ascribed to him. This is not the assumption or opinion of conservative writers only. Bleek, whose work is revised and sanctioned by Wellhausen, admits it to be a matter of the highest probability that no inconsiderable number of the Psalms are due to his authorship.† He also, with others, largely accepts the inscriptions which are prefixed to them. According to Canon Cook, a judicious and able writer, it was never held that the entire Psalter

---

* Cook's Introduction, p. 150.
† "Einleitung in das alte Testament . . . besorgt von J. Wellhausen." Sect. 221. Berlin, 1886.

was the work of the King; and he says that, in the time of the Maccabees, the completion of the Book was ascribed to Nehemiah. He thinks that a large proportion of the two closing books (out of the five Books composing the Psalter) belong to the period of or following the Exile.* But of the three Psalms most pointedly referable to the Messiah, two (xxii., cx.) are Davidic. He shows how the conclusive objections to the theory which refers the Psalms to the Maccabean age are sustained by various advanced German writers, and Bleek holds that no Psalm can be shown to be later than Nehemiah. But the master idea of the whole argument is not so much that such and such Psalms were produced at such and such an era, as that the Book at large is the product of that influence which stamps it, like the other books of Holy Scripture, as embodying a Divine revelation.

On this point of antiquity, it is more than enough if a large portion of the Psalms are ascribable to King David. I venture, however, to offer two suggestions. First, the Psalms come to us through a channel supplied by the kingdom of Judah, not the kingdom of Israel. If they had been largely

---

* Cook's Introduction, p. 156. The Books are Psalms i.-xli., xlii -lxxii., lxxiii.-lxxxix., xc.-cvi., cvii.-cl.

composed after the severance of the ten tribes from the two, would they not have presented some more definite indication of that severance? Now, the name of Israel is the name, under which in the Psalms the chosen people are described. We have this name repeated twenty-six times. The name of Judah was likely, it may be supposed, after the schism, to become the prevailing and distinctive name. It would so continue after the captivity and dispersion of the ten tribes, and as long as their remnants continued to maintain any serious and systematic rivalry with the southern kingdom. Yet, throughout the Psalter, we never find the name of Judah mentioned in this paramount sense. Jerusalem is mentioned seventeen times, and Sion thirty-eight, together fifty-five times. But the name of Judah only occurs ten times, and never with this paramount significance. It is mentioned either together with Israel (Ps. lxxvi. 1; cxiv. 2), or in conjunction with other tribes, as with Ephraim and Manasseh in Ps. lx. 7, and cviii. 8, or with Sion; but always locally or tribally. Could this have been so, if the Psalms had mainly been composed when Judah was the only acknowledged name for the elect people, and Israel was a stranger, often an enemy, always the symbol of a rival and apparently, from the character of its priesthood,* a degraded worship?

Secondly: the one great deliverance commemorated in the Psalms (as also, I understand, in the later Jewish Liturgies), is the deliverance from Egypt. See, for example, Psalms lxviii., lxxii., lxxx., lxxxi., cv., cvi., cxiv., cxxxv., cxxxvi. Could this have been the case, if the Book was unknown until the time when, between the people and their earlier past, there arose up a frightful spectre? I refer to the terrible experience of the Captivity in Babylon.

And yet, surely, there were incidents attendant upon that Captivity, which might have carved upon the Jewish mind recollections yet deeper in some respects than those of Egypt. In that country, if their treatment had been cruel and degrading, yet they must upon the whole have flourished, inasmuch as they grew there from a family into a people. But the Babylonish captivity entailed, firstly, the loss of what was not only an ancestral home, but the local seat of the Divine promise to their race; secondly, the loss of the worship divinely ordained, and attached to the temple of Jerusalem; thirdly, the loss of the kingly line, and of that prized nationality, in and by which they were preferred before all the

* 1 Kings xii. 31; xiii. 33.

nations of the earth. Is it then conceivable, if the Psalms in general owed their origin to the time of the Captivity, that the composers of them should, in numerous and conspicuous cases, have dwelt so long and so often on the details of the Egyptian bondage, and should never but once and briefly have made reference, specific indeed but narrow, to the one recent catastrophe, choosing rather to go back to the centuries dimmed, in comparison, by the interval of a thousand years?

It seems more than possible that this argument may be decisively supported by that portion of the Book of Jeremiah, which distinctly prophesies, not long before the Captivity, that a time is coming when the servitude in Egypt shall cease to be the one commanding recollection of the Hebrews, and its place shall be taken by the Exile in Babylon.

"Therefore, behold, the days come, saith the Lord, that it shall no more be said, The Lord liveth, that brought up the children of Israel out of the land of Egypt;
"But, the Lord liveth, that brought up the children of Israel from the land of the north, and from all the lands whither he had driven them: and I will bring them again into their land that I gave unto their fathers." *

The arguments, drawn from general features and from historical probability,

* Jer. xvi. 14, 15.

respecting the antiquity of the Books of the Old Testament, are in some degree common to the Torah, or Books of Moses, and the Psalms. The Psalms have, however, the benefit of the admission I have cited from the leader of the negative school in our own day, that a considerable number are probably from the pen of David. And there are also points in which reasoning, available to show the antiquity of the Torah, has an enhanced force for the Psalms.

We see, for example, that the history of the Israelites, from the conquest of Canaan to the Captivity, is upon the whole a history of a decaying faith. This is exhibited in the original demand for the change to a monarchy from that earlier form of government by Judges, which powerfully suggested the presence and providence of the Almighty, by leaving unoccupied the place upon earth most symbolical of Him. It was shown by the increased wickedness of the kings, and by the enlarged and developed office of the Prophets. For these were like an army of reserve in support of the Divine dispensation, which takes its position on the field of battle in the hour of need.

It is also observed by Sack,* that in the

---

* "Die altjüdische Religion im Übergange vom Bibelthume zum Talmudismus, von Israel Sack." Berlin, 1889. Einleitung, pp. 13, *seqq.*

period succeeding the exile the original creative force of the Hebrew spirit died out, and that, as formalism advanced, the sectarian lines of party were sharpened and deepened. In both these tracts of history, the spirit and voice of the Book of Psalms throw us back upon antiquity, and even upon a distant antiquity. They seem to be manifestly the product as of a school, so probably of an age, of living, energetic faith. And they are not less eminently notable for the harmony which pervades the religious community. "Jerusalem is built as a city, that is at unity in itself." *

III.—THEIR CONTENTS.

Let us now look for a moment at the contents of this Book, which are such as to fasten our wonder upon them, and to leave little room for any surprise that they should have established for themselves, in collective worship and in personal devotion, the place to which no parallel is elsewhere to be found in the experience of the human race. And, on the other hand, I shall not fail to notice in their proper place the objections which some have urged against the Book of Psalms.

* Psalm cxxii. 3.

The multiplication of divinities under the system which we term polytheism, had tended to establish everywhere a system of what are termed national gods. These act within the sphere of a particular race or country: they are open to the competition of other deities, when through migration or conquest these spheres happen to overlap. They do not claim the allegiance of other races, or show care or, so to speak, responsibility, for their welfare.

I do not indeed deny, but should be forward to assert, that while, in the early stages of historic antiquity, this nationalizing process seems to harden more and more with the gradual accretions of legendary tradition, we can trace among the mythologies, in various degrees of faintness or clearness, the older idea of a supreme God; of a belief in one Ruler of the universe, anterior and superior to these multiform powers. We find in many cases disguised resemblances of that original belief; but it is most commonly with such dislocation of its elements, such exaggerations, such intrusion of ideas foreign to it, as to defy all attempts, at least in the present state of knowledge, to ascend the channel upwards to the source. The schemes become so complex, as to defy any rational account of the original deviation: even when their basis is found to lie in the several powers of external nature, which were not known to be connected by any common tie, but which received the names of gods, and were combined into religious systems. These popular gods became realities in two senses; first, subjectively, because as they were accepted in the minds of men, the associations connected with them became a source and spring of human action; secondly, because the images, under which they came to be represented, gave them a real existence at least in the material sphere. It is, therefore, natural that the Psalms, in phrases concerning deity, should not be confined to the One God, but should say, for example, that among the gods there is none like Him, or should exhort the worshippers to give thanks unto the God of gods.*

Yet no reader of the Psalms can fail to see that they are strictly, unconditionally, and exclusively monotheistic. God is undoubtedly the God of Israel, and the worshippers properly describe Him in the terms, which most closely correspond with His relation to themselves. There seems to be a great mixture of the terms of Elohim and Jehovah, and in none of the five Books is the use of the properly Hebrew name exclusive.† But, without drawing any argument

---

* Ps. lxxxvi. 8; cxxxvi. 2. See Exodus xv. 11.
† Cook's Introd., p 149.

from this intermixture, the Psalms make it plain that the God whom they adore is from everlasting, and is the God, not of Palestine, but of the whole world: "Sing unto God, O ye kingdoms of the earth; O sing praises unto the Lord; who sitteth in the heavens over all from the beginning."* And His eye and care are over all men. "O praise the Lord all ye heathen: praise Him all ye nations. For His merciful kindness is ever more and more towards us; and the truth of the Lord endureth for ever."†

No doubt the "Lord" is represented as having special relations with and special care for Israel. But these are relations of affection, not of exclusion. A Psalm declares indeed—

"He shall choose out an heritage for us; even the worship of Jacob, whom he loved."

But the very same Psalm had already sounded the trumpet note—

"O clap your hands together, all ye people; O sing unto God with the voice of melody: for the Lord is high, and to be feared; He is the great king upon all the earth." ‡

Among the notes, then, of the supreme position of the Psalms, and of the religion to which they belonged, we find this idea of the one God, who is also the universal

* Ps. lxviii. 32-3. † Ps. cxvii. ‡ Ps. xlvii. 4, and 1-2.

God, and the universal Governor of men, and who thereby stands broadly distinguished from what we find to be the character of the polytheistic systems and of their heads; namely, divinity restrained by limits of the races or countries of antiquity.

But the form of the Almighty, thus divested of the limitations of mere nationality, and exhibited in the majesty of perfect Oneness and Omnipotence, revealed itself through the Psalms in other and more tender aspects. His care for the poor and for the stranger might be learned from the books of the law, and may be traced in other religions among the remnants of true Theism. Still, that is a function of government only, though of benevolent government, and it is compatible with the idea of immeasurable remoteness. But in the Psalms is developed with singular force and beauty the idea of Omnipotence in the attitude of nearness to man: and, more conspicuously still, of nearness to the individual man. In Heaven, and in the Underworld, and at the extremities of earth, "even there also shall Thy hand lead me, and Thy right hand shall hold me." *

The presence thus brought near is not, as in Exodus,† a consuming, but a soothing and sustaining presence.‡ When thus

* Ps. cxxxix. 6-9.   † Chap. xix. 12, 13, 21.   ‡ Ps. xxiii.

brought near, the Almighty is invested in relation to us with all those capacities of action and of sympathy, which fill in human nature the department of the affections. In the mouth of the objector, this is termed anthropomorphism. I do not presume to say that there is not in it some prefiguration of the Messiah, made in all such things like as we are. But that there is no deflection from the loftiness of the monotheistic idea we know from this, that the same people, who gave utterance to the Psalms, have been the most rigid and lofty in their definitions of the Godhead. As when it is said by Maimonides that with God "there is neither folly nor wisdom, like the wisdom of a wise man; neither sleep nor waking; neither anger nor laughter; neither joy nor sorrow; neither silence nor speech, like the speech of the sons of men."* Yet it is He that is not only the guardian of His people, but as it were their sentinel; and not of His people only, but of every one among them, as truly and as much as of the whole. In truth, the two threads of national and of personal

* Maimonides, "Yad Hachazakah." Transl. Bernard, Cambridge, 1832, p. 39. Declarations not less remarkable are to be found in the *More Nebuchim*, or "Guide of the Perplexed." See also the work of Dr. Ginsburg on the Kabbala, pp. 87-9 (London, Longmans, 1864).

Providence are so intertwined in the Psalms that they scarcely can be severed. "He will not suffer thy foot to be moved, and He that helpeth thee will not sleep;" and then in the very next verse, by a transition not less gentle than complete, "Behold, He, that keepeth Israel, shall neither slumber nor sleep." There is no detail too minute for describing the closeness of this protection: "He is thy defence upon thy right hand;" "The Lord shall preserve thy going out and thy coming in: from this time forth for evermore."* But no mere selection can rightly convey a picture of the close and intimate care, which this and so many others of the Psalms describe in setting forth the attitude of the Almighty towards His worshippers.

I will not quit this portion of the subject without quoting a remarkable testimony to the elevation of the Psalter from a recent critic generally negative, but one who makes his affirmative declarations with an exemplary sincerity and fervor. He speaks of the Psalter as follows: "It is, as a whole, the expression and fruit of the principles of the Jewish religion, as they existed in the minds of pious Israelites. Its one great theme is the clinging of the human spirit to God. In joy and sorrow, in victory

* Ps. cxxi. 3, 4, 5, 8.

and defeat, in moods of saintliness or sin, the spirit of the poor earthly wayfarer here pours out its plaint and prayer to the God of its life. . . . . What exultation is here, for high days of victory and joy! What touching moans of penitence! What childlike cries for help! What entreaties from the soul that can only say, 'out of the depths I have cried unto Thee!' What delightful confidences between the trustful spirit, and the Shepherd who leadeth by the green pastures and the still waters!"*

I must not altogether pass by the Messianic Psalms. These are the songs which show, by the adaptation of their language to Him and to His office, either that their composers had a prevision of His coming, or that such prevision was conveyed into their strain by the higher influence which prompted it. It is not necessary here to debate their number. Suffice it to specify Psalms ii., xxi., xxii., xlv., lxxii., cx. And it is sufficiently plain that the principle of prophecy, which is involved in them, whether conscious or unconscious to the composer, is the same which belongs to the other predictions and prefigurations in the books of the Old Testament. But they differ from, and go beyond, the rest in this important particular. The primitive religion descends

* Seven Lectures by the Rev. J. P. Hopps; vii. p. 33.

through them, as it were by an inner conduit. The great and cardinal facts of the lapse of man from righteousness, and of the need and promise of a Redeemer, were embodied by the Psalms in the perpetual public worship of the Temple; they thus became part of the open, common inheritance of all; and were systematically forced, so to speak, upon the attention of the people, that they might come into personal and conscious appropriation of this most precious and absolutely central part of their covenanted privileges.

When the foot of the Greek first, and afterwards of the Roman, trod the streets of Jerusalem; when the treasures of the Hebrew books were unlocked to the Gentile world through the Septuagint; then there happened, we may justly assume, one of two things. There was, as we know upon strong heathen testimony, before the advent of our Lord, an universal and traditional expectation in the East that a great power was to arise in Judæa and to subdue the world. How came it that so remarkable a conception, foreign to the cultivated communities of the Greek and the Italian peninsulas, and apparently menacing the continuance of the Roman dominion, should at this time have been prevalent in the East? The East had, indeed, through a long series of centuries, supposed itself entitled to the mastery of the world : hence the wild expedition of Darius into Scythia, and the repeated conflicts of Persia with the Greeks. It is not strange that this heritage should in some shape or other be reclaimed, for ideas of this kind are tenacious of life, and easy of revival. But what is at first sight most strange is, the choice of the spot from which deliverance was to proceed. It was not from any of the seats of ancient power, the fame of which was still on record; but from among the small, isolated, and undistinguished people who inhabited Palestine, and whose brief appearance on the stage of human affairs as conquerors, in the time of King David, was so slight in limit and in duration, as to have inscribed no mark upon the page of general history. It had passed away, like the old empire of the Hittites. The Jews were also a people, whose manners and institutions repelled rather than attracted the sympathy of the world. One supposition, explanatory of this remarkable expectation, might be that it had lived on from prehistoric times in feebleness and obscurity, but had come to the front when the East felt the hard hand of power pressing on it from Rome, and welding it for the first time by a permanent system into uniformity of servitude or inferiority, from which it panted for deliverance. But it seems more probable that the Jewish Scriptures, which had for two centuries become known by translation into Greek, were themselves the fountain-head of this most remarkable anticipation; and in that case its popular promulgation would seem most probably to have been due, in an eminent degree, to the Messianic Psalms, which were, of all the available evidence, the part most in the eye and mind of the people.

Such being, in outline, the presentation of God to man in the Book of Psalms, let us consider in its turn the manner in which they present man to God. Now this may be set forth in a multitude of particulars, but they are all capable of being summed into one. For we have seen that the Psalms are a book of spiritual communion, not only between God and man, not only between God and His Church, or especially chosen people, but also, and even pre-eminently, between God and the individual man.

As it is the fashion of the day to assert for the sacred books of other religions a kind of parity with the Old Testament, I ask the reader to spend a few moments on this subject.

No doubt there are points at which resemblance may be traced between the Hebrew devotions and those of the outer world: not those of the outer world generally, for from the Greek mind, as represented by the Greek literature, devotion, properly so called, has disappeared; the rise of intellect, sad and strange as this may sound, was the fall of piety. But let it be granted that in the Vedas, for example, and in the Babylonian Hymns, there are points of contact with the Psalms. Do those points of contact run along the whole line? are they continuous, or are they isolated? Is it coincidence, or is it a sort of tangential contact only, or one which reminds us of the definition of a point as that which has position but not magnitude in space?

May not those hymns be described as belonging only to the idea of dependence upon the Deity—to the power and grandeur which exists on one side, the misery and weakness on the other? This is perhaps what is called the religious sentiment, the religion of which we have a subjective need, and which we are now constantly (and doubtless in good faith) assured is not to disappear on the submergence of positive religion and its institutions. But does this give us anything near a true conception of the Psalms? They are based upon the idea, not of dependence only, but of sympathy and communion. Yes, for the work of spiritual discipline, the human soul is there almost lifted upwards, as St. Paul was, into the third heaven, and meets the Creator as son meets father, face to face. It is not possible, perhaps, to carry this idea farther, than it is carried in the Psalms. It is certainly not woven into a closer tissue in Thomas à Kempis, after fourteen centuries of Christian ideas and practices. We approach to it in the Prophets, when, through Isaiah, the Almighty invites us to a pleading (Is. i. 18), " Come now, and let us reason together." * But can we, even in idea, press it further or lift it higher than in that marvellous expostulation of the forty-fourth Psalm. It defies the test of extract or quotation. From the fifth verse to the end it is a sustained note of moving, sorrowing appeal, lifted as far above the level of any merely human effort known to us as the flight of the lark, "hard by the sun," is lifted above the swallow, when it foresees the storm and skims the surface of the ground. Such, as set forth in the Psalms are the inward exercises of the individual soul.

Not that the stamp set upon the Psalms is uniform: it is highly diversified. Take the noble first Psalm, which opens the Book. It sets forth in one part (verses 3 and 4) with a tender beauty, in another

* See also Ezek. xviii. 25, 29.

with strong and stern denunciation, the positions of the righteous and of the wicked before God. But it sets them forth, as it were, from the outside. So, again, many of the Psalms, dealing with the Israelites as a whole, have for their theme national deliverance and glory. But let us turn to the penitential Psalms, and most of all to the fifty-first, in which King David * sounds the lowest depths of sorrow and shame for sin, and has provided for the penitent of every age and every character the medicine that his case required. On these Psalms as a whole, on this Psalm in particular, and, again on the thirty-eighth Psalm, most of all in its first moiety, let us fasten our attention for a moment. Have modern learning and research succeeded in extracting from all the sacred books of all the ancient religions of the world anything like, I do not say a parallel, but an ever so remote approach to them? The great discourse of our Lord to Nicodemus, in the third chapter of St. John, might find in these compositions a basis broad enough to sustain the whole of His startling doctrine, "except a man be born again, he cannot see the kingdom of God." †

* Some critics argue, not without some reason on their side, that the two last verses are an exilic addition.
† John iii. 3.

Penitence thus lying at the door of the process by which man is appointed to ascend to holiness, this golden book supplies, beyond all others, the types and aids for attaining it in all its stages. All that special class of virtues, which were unknown to the civilized world at the time when the Apostles preached them, had been here set forth in act a thousand years before, and stored up for use, first within the narrow circle of the Jewish worship, and then in the Church, which claims, and which may yet possess, the wide world for its inheritance. Another standard of virtue indeed, and in itself a glorious one, the Greek and the Roman world possessed. They had their code of Justice, Fortitude, Temperance, and Wisdom. But this list of virtues contained no recognition of the terrible and world-wide fact of sin, and opened no road to the acquisition of powers capable of contending against it, and of casting down its strongholds to the ground. That road was to be opened by the Beatitudes of the Sermon on the Mount, and by the Faith, Hope, and Charity of St. Paul. Now, is there one of those Beatitudes which has not been, in its blossom or its germ, anticipated by the Psalms? Take the sanctification of sorrow in verse 4: so the Psalm instructs us, "Thy loving correction shall make me great"

(Ps. xviii. 35). Take the blessing of the meek (verse 5). So says the Psalmist: "Lord, I am not high-minded. I have no proud looks. I refrain my soul and keep it low. My soul is even as a weaned child." (Ps. cxxxi. 1, 3.) These are principles, not only which the ancient philosophies did not contain, but which they would have repudiated and contemned. Take again that blessing of satiety which is promised to "hunger and thirst" after righteousness; words which indicate such an adult age, such a fulness of growth and stature in the new man of the Christian system, that what was at first lesson from without has come to be appetite from within, and part of the untaught spontaneous working of a renewed humanity. But this idea is fully developed in the Psalms (xlii. 1, 2), "Like as the hart desireth the water brooks, so longeth my soul after Thee, O God. My soul is athirst for God, yea, even for the living God: when shall I come to appear before the presence of God." Even the doctrine of forgiveness, of doing good to enemies, to the growth of which the conditions of Hebrew life were less favorable, finds expression in the Psalms. Take xxxv. 12, 13: "They rewarded me evil for good. Nevertheless, when they were sick I put on sackcloth, and humbled my soul with fasting." And again, "If I have rewarded evil unto him that dealt friendly with me: yea, I have delivered him that without any cause is mine enemy" (Ps. vii. 4). It is, I submit, the general strain of the Psalms to which we should look. And who will deny that they habitually abound in humility, in penitential abasement, in the strong faith which is the evidence of things not seen, in fervor, self-mistrust, filial confidence towards God? These and all kindred qualities they develop in what, for want of a better word, I will term their innerness. Their tones come from the inmost heart, and, not with a rude familiarity, yet with a wonderful nearness, they seem to seek the response, if the phrase may be used without irreverence, from the inner heart of God Himself.

All this is severed, as a whole, by an immeasurable distance from the language, ideas, and mental habits of pagan antiquity. What we find there of religion associated with intellectual culture turns upon the external relations between God and man, as between sovereign and subject, or master and dependent. The prehistoric verse of Homer abounds in prayers. They are not such commonly as we should use, yet they indicate fully these external relations. But in the life of later, of classical, Greece, prayer seems wholly to have lost its force and place as a factor in human life.

Again, in the "Odyssey" of Homer we have remaining traces of the personal relation between man and God. In the intercourse of Athenè with Odysseus, and reversely in her action on the minds of the guilty suitors, there are distinct traces of the working of a Divine force within the soul of man. I do not remember to have found anything like this in the later classical literature. But the development of the principle and idea of a communion with God, operative on human feeling, thought, and action, is the standing and central thought of the Psalms. And it is probable that, the more fixedly we regard them, the more of their distinctive marks we shall perceive, even as the stars in heaven multiply to the gazing eye. The pervading idea of a living communion with the Most High, the communion which both gives and takes, exhibits and fulfils itself in many ways. One of them is the use of intercessory prayer; a trait conspicuously absent from the numerous and interesting prayers of Homer. Another is that, while full of warm personal interests they persistently hold up the banner of a righteousness apart from and above all personal interests whatever. Another is that the affections, alienated by sin, have returned to their allegiance, and are arrayed on the side of the Most High. The testimonies of God are the "very joy" of the Psalmist's heart. It is all his desire that the Divine will should have free course and be glorified upon earth. The glory of God has become to him a profound personal interest. "Set up thyself, O God, above the heavens; and thy glory above all the earth." Sentiments of this type are, I apprehend, hardly to be found outside the precinct of the Hebrew race.

I will only note, in passing, before quitting this subject, two remaining characteristics; the height of that sacredness which the Psalms attach to the claims of the poor; and their sense of the utter worthlessness of all ceremonial observances, though commanded, except in connection with the service of the will, and purification of the heart.

IV.—THE OBJECTIONS TAKEN TO THEM.

Referring to what has been said elsewhere on the presence of a human element in Holy Scripture, I will now say a few words on the special objection which is lodged against the Psalms.

Let me first endeavor to reduce the question to its true dimensions. The criticism is not here, as it might be in some cases of books claiming to be sacred, that they are feeble, or fanciful, or remote from human interests, or that large veins of clay run through such true metal as they contain. The Psalms, in their sublimity and in their sympathy, so immeasurably divine and so intensely human, are proof against all such criticism, which would be only cavil. The only dart which really rings upon their coat of mail, is the dart which carries the reproach of their severe and unmeasured denunciation of enemies.

And first, in order to disembarrass the question of matter which appears to be extreme and exceptional, I will refer to the verse which represents the *ne plus ultra* of the difficulty, as it stands in the Prayer-book Version of the Psalms; in respect to which we pay a certain price for its incomparable majesty and beauty, in the shape of occasional though rare shortcomings as to accuracy. The Prayer-book gives verses 21, 22, of Psalm cxxxix., as follows:—

"Do not I hate them, O Lord, that hate thee: and am not I grieved with those that rise up against thee?

"Yea, I hate them right sore: even as though they were mine enemies."

Which seems to say, "I have a reserved

stock of special and superlative hatred for those who have not only sinned in general, but have sinned against me in particular." But this notion is completely put aside in the translation direct from the Hebrew as it stands in the Authorized, and also in the Revised Version, where the second of the two verses runs :—

"I hate them with a perfect hatred ; I count them mine enemies."

This seems not to set up the selfish feeling, about offence personally received, above the sentiment of indignation and resentment against wickedness ; but to say only, "All that I might feel against a personal enemy, all that natural exasperation would suggest, I discharge upon the enemies of God." But the sentiment concerning them has already been expressed in terms not admitting of enlargement. "I hate them with a perfect hatred." And this brings the objection to a point. It is that this unmeasured detestation and invocation of wrath by man even upon God's enemies cannot be justified, and is not to be referred to divine inspiration.

Now let us notice, in the first place, that the general tone of the Psalms concerning enemies is not aggressive, but defensive. A sense of trouble and danger from the might of experienced or impending assault, and an appeal to God for protection, furnish the staple sentiment of the Book. I quote a single instance, which is a fair sample of the whole of this class of passages, from Psalm lvi. 1, 2 :—

> "Be merciful unto me, O God, for man goeth about to devour me: he is daily fighting and troubling me.
> "Mine enemies are daily in hand to swallow me up: for they be many that fight against me, O thou Most High."

Let those who question the assertion I have made, that this passage has a character typical of the whole, refer (among other places) to Psalms v. 8; vi. 7; vii. 5; xviii. 27, *passim;* lvi. 9; lix. 1; lxix. 4; cxviii. 11, 12; cxxxviii. 7; cxliii. 9.

But undoubtedly a certain number of passages are not defensive, they are denunciatory; such as liv. 5, 7; lix. 10; xcii. 11; cxliii. 12. I will recite this last verse in full, for it brings into view the sentiment which forms the base of all these passages: "And of thy goodness slay mine enemies, and destroy all them that vex my soul, *for I am thy servant.*" If we put these words into paraphrase, the Psalmist pleads that he is engaged in the service of God; that in this service he is assailed and hindered; that, powerless in himself, he appeals to the source of power; and that he invokes upon the assailants and hinderers of the Divine work the Divine vengeance, even to their extinction.

We have, then, to consider these denunciatory passages, first, as they were employed by their authors; secondly, as they are now presented to us for our own use in the services of the Church, or in private devotion.

Under the first head, let me observe as follows. There is not one of these passages which tampers with truth or justice; they are aimed only at sin, to blast and wither it. "Lead me, O Lord, in Thy righteousness, because of mine enemies" (Ps. v. 8). This is the universal strain. All these passages are strokes delivered with the sword of righteousness, in its unending warfare with iniquity. Nor is there one among them, of which it can be shown that it refers to any personal feud, passion, or desire. Everywhere the Psalmist speaks in the name of God, on behalf of His word and will.

But it may still be urged, that such denunciations are excessive in degree, that they are too severe and savage, and that they are not suitable for the mouth of man.

With respect to their severity I suggest, and if need be contend, that we, in our ignorance and weakness, are no fit judges of the extent to which the wisdom of the Almighty may justly carry the denunciation, even by the mouth of man, and the punishment of guilt.

Man, and even civilized man, contemplates with much equanimity the taking of human life for the occasions which he deems sufficient. He knows that in all wars one party must be guilty, and that in most or many wars neither have had a justification for the wholesale bloodshed, which floods the path of destruction that they necessarily follow. Life, which man did not give and cannot restore, he takes away, for the repression of crime, with general, though not unanimous, approval. It is also taken, even now, in most Christian countries, through duels for private injury or insult; and it is but recently that public opinion in our own country has become repugnant to the practice. But the scruples, which for ourselves we so easily thrust aside, become active, feverish, and even violent, when, in a world to the abundant wickedness of which our own practice witnesses, the Ruler of that world, who gave life for use, and who sees and judges its abuse, is to be arraigned before our mock tribunal; and we, who cannot and do not rightly guide, each of us, our own action, are to undertake to determine

His. 'And this, when we have not fully learned, and cannot measure, either the deep and frightful depravity of the Canaanitish nations, or the purposes with which Penalty descends from on high. We know not whether it comes in mercy to correct the growth of evil before it shall become incurable, and whether, or how far, when opportunity has been exhausted here, resources may still have been held in reserve on behalf of persons placed as they were, to be expended for good in the great Elsewhere. To pronounce verdicts upon these terrible denunciations may be impious; and is surely, at the least, unreasonable.

> " And who art thou, that on the bench would sit,
> To judge what is a thousand miles removed,
> With the brief vision of a single span ? " *

There is certainly more claim to substance in the objection, which urges that these denunciations are unsuitable for man. But here I should interpose the question, To what man? The wonderful nature, in which we have been created, is in nothing more wonderful than in the diversity of the conditions under which it has to subsist and work, on its road from embryo to perfection. As those stages accumulate, the moral code becomes multiform and involved.

* Dante, " Parad." xix. 81.   Pollock's translation.

In simpler forms of life, and in earlier stages of society, the roads between right and wrong were short, broad, and clear; like as were then the dividing spaces of the battle-field, whereas contending hosts are now severed by miles, and almost leagues, from one another.

But, further, the Psalmists, and the nation to which they belonged, lived under a different dispensation from ours. If we accept the Scriptures, that nation held a divine commission to establish the right and to put down the wrong, in a sense in which no such commission is now given. For us it is enough to hope that at any given juncture we may be doing the will of God; but what we hope, they knew; and sight for them was mixed with faith in a degree and mode remote from the spirit of our later, and in this respect, perhaps, higher training. They were accustomed to what may be termed short accounts with the Divine Justice; and to reward or suffering as the immediate consequences, and, therefore, as the direct attestations, of the judgment of God upon the moral conduct of man. The responsibility, which is for us diffused and indefinite, was for them concentrated and palpable. But, besides this, they had the great standing institution of prophecy; and the king in whose ears Nathan's words had thundered, "Thou art the man," might well feel that his own contact was a close one with the mind of the Almighty, and that he might upon occasion speak his very strongest words under guidance from on High.

I do not pursue farther these remarks, which are no more than tentative and approximate. But I do not find myself justified in the assumption that we are in all cases to have a complete cognizance of the conditions under which the Psalms give judgment upon the unrighteous, or are intended to arrive at final judgments on the question what the Jews might, and what they might not, suitably be commissioned by the Almighty to denounce.

More immediately are we concerned in the question as to the place held in Christian devotion, and especially in public ritual, by the denunciatory passages of the Psalms. It is one question what these denunciations were for the Jew; it is another, and entirely distinct, what they are for us. But the answer to this objection, I apprehend, lies near to hand. All scruple, at least all rational or plausible scruple in this matter, seems to rest upon the supposition that the passages are aimed at creatures, who have characters mixed between good and evil, and who therefore are not presumptively fit subjects for our unmixed, undiscriminating denunciation. But can any one reasonably suppose that these declarations are, in the mind and sense of the Christian Church, directed against any human enemy? Our human enemies, if we are so unhappy as to have any, are not the most watchful, the most subtle, the most destructive of our foes. "For we wrestle not against flesh and blood, but against . . . . the rulers of the darkness of this world.* But the Holy Scripture and the Christian religion teach, and our human experience largely testifies, that there are spirits whose meat and drink, so to speak, it is to extend the domain of evil, to deepen corruption, to destroy happiness by destroying innocence, which is its base; to add both in range and in intensity to the misery and the sin which have made the world so sad. If this be so, then I contend that to pray for the abolition or paralysis of their work and of its agents, and this especially when we meet as Christians to set forth solemnly the collective needs and aspirations of mankind, is a practice which speaks for itself, and requires neither justification nor apology.

Apart altogether from the question, what may be the value or completeness of the foregoing defensive suggestions, I would

* Eph. vi. 12.

remind my readers that they relate not to the main body of the question respecting the Psalms, but to a portion of it which is limited and exceptional. The Psalms, like other productions, are to be judged by their general character. I do not perceive how, if we approach this question on the grounds and in the spirit of reason, it is possible for a person so approaching it to set aside the mass of evidence, which establishes the unparalleled and unapproached position of the Book in its antiquity and use, in its pure and noble theology, and in a moral and spiritual character witnessed afresh by the judgment and practice of each succeeding age. And, if the several parts of this evidence link themselves into a compact and harmonious whole, it is not reason, but unreason in the mask of reason, which declines or omits to acknowledge the presumption thence arising, that the Book is at a level indefinitely higher than has been reached by the unassisted faculties of man, and that the power which raised it to that level can only be Divine. Such a conclusion will survive even the approving reference in Ps. cxxxvii. 9, to a practice of savage warfare. Were it true that the image of gold had feet of clay, we might indeed be perplexed by the combination; but would not this be just, as we often are perplexed by other combinations, presented to us in the providential government of the world? And not only in the providential government of the world, but in the fulfilment of our personal relations with other men. Yet we do not put an end on that account to such relations: nor do we cease to believe in God because we, such as we are—God save the mark—cannot comprehend the reason, or even discern the rightfulness, of all He does. In like manner, so neither can we refuse to admit sufficient evidence of an origin more than human for the Psalms on the ground that we see only through a glass darkly, and that they present incidental features analogous in principle to those which in other departments our experience brings before us.

The Mosaic Legislation.

The Mosaic Legislation.

THE legislative Books of the Pentateuch, from Exodus to Deuteronomy, may be contemplated in the light, either (1) of their credentials, or (2) of their character and contents.

The Christian Church, which had heretofore regarded them as an integral and instructive part of the Divine Revelation, is now challenged by the voices of numerous critics to defend them. Champions in this cause are not wanting; and it is not to be supposed that the learned in linguistic studies have arrived at unanimous and final conclusions in these grave matters. If we compare their studies, as to unanimity, continuity, and ascertained progress, with that of the natural sciences, the comparison will be not at all to their advantage. Their services are not, however, to be unduly disparaged. What is understood to be at issue is, the date and authorship of the Books in the form in which we now have them. These are contested by the negative school on grounds of language and style, upon which none can properly attempt to follow or to judge them, unless when equipped with the same special knowledge. They also allege, as parts of the destructive argument, that the Books contain anachronisms, contradictions, statements disproved by history.

They have recently been challenged by Dr. Cave * to set forth a plain and distinct statement of these difficulties, such as might bring the allegations in some degree within the circles of knowledge and of judgment, for us who are not experts but are supposed to be endued with ordinary intelligence. They are also invited to state what meaning they assign to the standing phrase, "And the Lord spake unto Moses," which with its variants occurs, it may be observed, no less than thirty times in the twenty-seven chapters of Leviticus. And, finally, they are invited by Dr. Cave to show in plain terms the reasons why it is unreasonable to suppose that the Books (either in their present state or otherwise) were contemporaneous with the events described and grew up one by one along with those events.

It seems but common equity that we, who stand outside the learned world, and who find operations are in progress, which are often declared to have destroyed the

* *Contemporary Review*, April 1890, pp. 537–551.

authority of these ancient Books, should be supplied, as far as may be, with available means of rationally judging the nature and grounds of the impeachment. And it is unfortunate that this has been little thought of; and that, while we are, it may almost be said, drenched with the deductions and conclusions of the negative critics, it is still so difficult, in multitudes of instances, to come at any clear view of the grounds on which they build. The matters of style and language we must contentedly take upon trust; but anachronism, contradiction of history, contradiction in the Books themselves, ought to be more or less within our cognizance. And there are many arguments of historical verisimilitude and likelihood, which are in no sense the exclusive property of specialism.

Even within the compass of the Torah, a distinction has been drawn by some eminent critics (by Eichhorn, for example), in their writings on the canon of the Old Testament;* who have assigned the legislative portions to Moses himself, and the historical parts to scribes acting under his direction, or at a later time. It does not appear

* A most convenient summary of the history of critical opinion on the Pentateuch is supplied by Bleek *cum* Wellhausen in the *Einleitung* (Ed. 1886), sects. 13–17. Wellhausen adds another review at the close of the volume in this edition.

easy to show why this singular intermixture of the two should have been made, unless by or under the direction of the lawgiver himself. The tangled occupations of his evidently hard-pressed life would account for a form of authorship, which is not in itself at all convenient. But the ordinary reader will not fail to observe that it is the legislation, for which in the sacred text itself the claim is constantly made of being due to direct communication from above,* while no corresponding assertion in general accompanies the historical recitals. Speaking at large, every imaginable difference has prevailed among the critics themselves as to the source, date, and authorship of the Books. But on the whole, the negative movement has become bolder in its assertions as it proceeded, and has brought them gradually towards later epochs: to Samuel, to the age of David, to the severance of the kingdoms, to Josiah, to the Captivity, and even to those who followed it. The affirmative side has been also stoutly maintained,† not without the admission of particular additions and interpolations in the received text. The distinction between substantial authorship, and final editorship, has been largely recognized by writers of celebrity

---

* So Wellhausen in the *Einleitung*, sect. 18, p. 40.
† *Ibid.* sect. 15.

and weight. Bleek himself, sustained by Wellhausen as late as 1886, held that Moses had a hand (*einen antheil*) in the Legislative Books. Many of the laws, they say at that date, are without sense or purpose, except in regard to circumstances which disappeared with the Mosaic period.* Several sections of this important work † are given to the indication of portions of the Books which must have been Mosaic. Further, we have this remarkable declaration. Though the entire Pentateuch in its present form should not have been the work of Moses, and though many laws are the product of a later age, still the legislation, in its spirit and character as a whole, is genuinely Mosaic; ‡ and that, in dealing with the Pentateuch, we stand, at least as to the three middle Books, upon historical ground,§ evidently meaning upon historical ground as opposed to that which is unauthenticated or legendary. Further, what is thus generally asserted of the spirit and character of the Pentateuchal laws, is asserted for an important share of them ‖ as to both the contents and even the form.

These statements—it would not be fair to

* *Ibid.* sect. 11. † 13–24.
‡ "*So muss doch die darin enthaltene gesetzgebung ihrem ganzen geiste und character nach echt mosaisch seyn.*"—*Ibid.*, sect. 22, p. 45.
§ *Ibid.* ‖ Sect. 23, p. 46.

call them admissions—go to the root of the whole matter, and seem to leave us in possession of that for which alone I contend; namely, that the heart and substance of the legislative and institutional system delivered to us in the Pentateuch is historically trustworthy. If this be so, it still remains highly important to distinguish by critical examination what, if any, particular portions of the work in their actual form may be open to question, either as secondary errors, or as developments appended to the original formation; but the citadel, so long victoriously held by faith and reason, both through Hebrew and through Christian ages, remains unassailed, and the documents of Holy Writ emerge substantially unhurt from the inquisitive and searching analysis of the modern time.

There is a later work of Wellhausen's (" Die composition des Hexateuch's und der Historischen Bücher:" Berlin, 1889) which minutely subdivides the Books into smaller portions, and refers these to their different authors, with a self-reliance which appears to be remarkable, but of which I am not a fit judge. I may observe, however, that this work has neither introduction nor conclusion, neither index nor table of contents, and that it resembles rather the promiscuous gatherings of a note-book, or rather, of two note-books crossing one another, discharged bodily into a printing-office, than a work of regular or scientific criticism. I must add that in certain cases, where the unity of the text is disputed upon grounds alike cognizable by us all, I find the conclusions of the author as disputable as they are confident. In other instances, numerous enough, assertions are made, as if they were oracles, without the slightest explanation, or any indication of their grounds. Examples of these methods may be found in the criticisms * on Genesis, and in the contradiction alleged to exist in the several accounts of Caleb and Joshua (Num. xxxii. 5, and Deut. i. 32–8).

A still more negative utterance, if I understand it rightly, is found in the "Prolegomena to the History of Israel," translated under the author's supervision, and accompanied with his article on Israel from the *Encyclopædia Britannica*. † This book, published since the edition of Bleek *cum* Wellhausen from which I have quoted, appears in a singular manner to contradict it, and announces that " the Mosaic history is not the starting-point for the history of ancient Israel, but for the history of Judaism." ‡ The distinction may not be

* Page 7. † Edinburgh: A. & C. Black, 1885.
‡ Preface by Professor Robertson Smith, p. v.

familiar to English readers, but the meaning seems to be that the Pentateuch had not, either in form or substance, any operative existence until after the Exile, when the ancient Israel is held to end, and Judaism to begin. A "Mosaic germ" only is admitted; and a germ is that which, like an unborn child, has no operative existence, but only the promise of producing one. According, then, to the showing of those who tender themselves as our guides, Israel lived on for nine hundred years, from the Exodus, and transmitted a peculiar faith, law, ritual, and nationality, without any legislative and constitutional system to uphold any one of them. This very startling proposition appears to me to do violence to reason not less glaringly, than any of the assertions ventured by the theologians in the days of their pride and power. Those writers are doubtless perfectly sincere, who represent this as a method of progressive revelation. But there are also persons who think that such a progressive revelation as this would for over two thousand years have palmed upon the whole Jewish and Christian world not only a heartless, but an impossible imposture. It is more immediately necessary to observe that the hypothesis is one reaching far beyond the province of specialism, and requiring to be tested at a number of points by considerations more broadly historical. Nor can I quit the subject without observing that it is extremely difficult to learn whether there exists any real standing ground, which the present negative writers mean not only to occupy but to hold. Almost any representation of their views may be either supported or contradicted by citing particular expressions from their works. All we can do is to dive as best we may into their conception of what Wellhausen rather singularly calls "the secrets" of his art.* Upon the whole, and taking the article on Israel in the *Encyclopædia Britannica* as the fairest exposition of his views, I infer that the present fashion is to believe in Moses, but to question even his connection with the Decalogue;† to allow him to have given or suggested a something, totally indefinite in its character, to the Israelites; and to hold that the materials of the legislative books gradually grew up out of material supplied upon occasion by the priests (like the "Answers of Experts,"‡ which supplied a contribution to the Code of Justinian) into a state which enabled editors, generally post-exilic, to reduce them to their present

* *Einleitung*, Ed. 1886, Vorwort.
† Wellhausen, Hist. Israel (Black), pp. 436, 509.
‡ Gibbon (Milman's ed.), iv. 193.

form. This scheme seems to be admirably represented by the words which Mr. Robbertson Smith quotes, on his own very high authority, as its gist. And this is the scheme to which I desire, on historical grounds, to demur.

At the same time it is undeniable that, even if the outside negative conclusions were still such as they were stated to be so lately as in 1886, yet the impression they had created was not of a similarly limited character. Whether owing to the predispositions of the time, or to a spirit latent in some of the critics, or to the reaction which is usually perceptible when certain ideas long cherished on one side have been found to require modification, there have been, as it were, exhalations from the recent inquiries, extending outwards in their effect much beyond the positive conclusions. An atmosphere has been diffused around us, and we habitually inhale it, which inspires a general uncertainty, leading to negation, with respect to the Mosaic Books. This causes us, not, perhaps, to believe (for this would imply and demand a rational process), but to feel towards these great foundation-books as if we believed, that, instead of being as to the heart and pith of them trustworthy, they were in the main untrustworthy; that they were compounded or composed at uncertain times, by uncertain authors, from uncertain materials; that even bad faith is to be traced in them; and that the question is not so much what particulars can be convicted of unauthenticity, as whether any particulars can be rescued from the general discredit of a mythical or legendary inception. It is against this vague, irrational, unscientific method of proceeding, that I would enter not a protest only, but a pleading. Whatever is to happen, let not Christians lose unawares either their faith, or that pillar of their faith which the great Books of the Old Testament always have supplied.

I have already made it clear that I yield, as matter of course, to the conclusions of linguists in their own domain, not only respectful attention, but provisional assent. That domain includes not only criticism strictly textual, but all that relates to style, and, in a word, whatever properties of any given writings are developed through the medium of the particular tongue in which they are composed. On the mere form of the Books they speak with a force which, as against us, the unlearned, is overwhelming. But, in the examinations directed to the matter as opposed to the form, their authority is of a less stringent character, and may even decline to zero. The historical aspects and relations which open out this field are not theirs exclusively, and we may canvass and question their conclusions, just as it is open to us to proceed with the conclusions of Macaulay or of Grote.

When it is attempted to bring down the date of the Pentateuch from the time of Moses, by whom the Books in various forms purport* to have been composed, to the period of the Babylonian captivity, and this not only as to their literary form, but as to their substance, the evident meaning and effect of the attempt is to divest them of an historical, and to invest them with a legendary character.

At the same time, it should be borne in mind that those who have not seen reason to adopt the negative theory above described, leave entirely open numerous questions belonging to the institutions of the Israelites. It is not extravagant to assume that laws given to them as a nomad people, and then subjected to the varying contin-

---

* For instance, as by the proem to Deuteronomy (i. 1): the recited orders of the Almighty to Moses that he should speak, followed by the speeches, *e. g.*, Lev. i. 1, Num. i. 1: the constant verbal report of words spoken to Moses when no other person (or in some cases Aaron only) was present: and the remarkable and high-toned injunctions in the later chapters of Deuteronomy which all through seem to have reference to a code of legislation preceding them.

gencies of history during many centuries, may or even must have required and received adaptation by supplement, development, or change in detail, which the appointed guides of the people were authorized and qualified to supply, not in derogation, but rather in completion and in furtherance of the work of Moses, which might still remain his in essence from first to last.

It is admitted, however, that the whole question must be tried on historical and literary grounds. On such grounds I seek to approach it, and to throw light upon it from some considerations of reason and probability, which appear to me to be of not inconsiderable cogency. By testing the subject in this way, we may come, in part at least, to learn by testing what in the main is fact, what in the main is speculation, and to a great extent fluctuating and changeful speculation.

First, it is never to be forgotten, that our point of departure is from the ground of established historic fact. The existence of Moses is even better and far better established than that (for example) of Lycurgus. We know Lycurgus in the main from the one great fact of his very peculiar institutions. They, such as we find them in historic times, compel us to presume his existence in a prehistoric time. Not only their high and elaborate organization, but their practical efficacy in separating and fencing off from the rest of Greece the Spartan community, reduces to something near absurdity any such supposition as that they were essentially no more than a late growth reached by imperceptible degrees. We know Moses as well from his institutions, which are by no means less peculiar, and which, as experience has shown, have been very far more durable. In the case of Moses, it happens that we have much evidence independent of, and anterior to, the institutions themselves in their historic form. Yet no one doubts either the existence of the Spartan lawgiver, or the general character of his personal work. If the form of the Books in which the Mosaic legislation reaches us be open to the suspicion of manipulation by scribes or editors, or if it suggest some suspicion of developments, how does this compare with the case of Lycurgus? About or from him we have no books at all; and yet it would be deemed irrational to doubt either the existence of the man, or the substance of the work performed by him.

The exodus from Egypt, the settlement in Palestine, the foundation there of institutions, civil and religious, which were endowed with a tenacity of life and a peculiarity of character beyond all example: these things are established by Scripture, but they are also established independent of Scripture. They constitute a *trinoda necessitas*, a threefold combination of fact, which, in order to make them intelligible and coherent, in order to supply a rational connection between cause and effect, require not only a Moses, but such a Moses as the Scripture supplies. They build up a niche, which the Scripture fills. At all times of history, and specially in those primitive times, when* the men made the governments, not the governments the men, these great independent historic facts absolutely carry with them the assumption of a leader, a governor, a legislator. All this simply means a Moses, and a Moses such as we know him from the Pentateuch.

And this leads us, I do not say to, but towards, the conclusion that whatever be the disparaging allegations of the critics, they may after all according to likelihood be found reasonable as to matters of form or of detail, but that the substance of the history is in thorough accordance with the historic bases that are laid for us in profane as well as in sacred testimony. If this be so, then we have also to bear in mind that

* So Montesquieu, "Grandeur et decadence des Romains," chap. i.

the phenomenon, which we have before us, is one so peculiar that it could only have been exhibited to the world as the offspring of a peculiar generating cause. A people of limited numbers, of no marked political genius, negative and stationary as to literature and art, maintain their absolutely separate existence for near a thousand years, down to the Captivity. They are placed in the immediate neighborhood, and subject to the frequent attacks, of the great Eastern monarchies, as well as of some very warlike neighbors. These attacks compromise their political independence, but do not prevent it from being recovered. They receive the impress of a character so marked that not even the Captivity can efface it; but, on the contrary, that searching trial helps to give a harder and sharper projection to its features. It retains its solidity and substance while everything else, including great political aggregations, such as the Hittite monarchy, becomes gradually fused in the surrounding masses; and this even when it has been subjected to conditions such as at Babylon, apparently sufficient to beat down and destroy the most obstinate nationalism. Can it be denied that this great historic fact, nowhere to be matched, is in thorough accordance with, and almost of itself compels us to presuppose, the existence from the outset of an elaborately detailed and firmly compacted system of laws and institutions, under which this peculiar discipline might subsist and work, so as gradually to shape, determine, and mature the character of the people?

If, apart from all questions of form and expression, the substance of the Mosaic law was given to the Israelites on their settlement in Palestine, such a provision, it may fearlessly be said, was in full accordance with the moral exigency of the case, and with the laws of historical probability. If on the other hand there was no Moses, or only a Moses who left nothing behind him, and who does not rank among the lawgivers of the world, if the Legislative Books represent a gradual and mythical accretion due mainly either to class interests or to the magnifying effect of distance, turned to account by invention either interested or credulous, then the hypothesis presented to us is, it may surely be contended, in violent discord with what, on principles of Providential government or of human good sense, the case would usually be held to have required.

In estimating the claim of the Old Testament to a divine origin, it is important to compare the legislation given by Moses with that of other ancient lawgivers, such, for example, as Solon, who enjoyed the light of a far more advanced civilization. Still, this comparison, if alone, would not fully bring out the reason of the case;' we must also match the Hebrew intellect, as measured by knowledge, art and manners, with the corresponding conditions among the other nations whose laws may be brought into the comparison. For if, with inferior tools and materials, a superior work was produced, it must surely be admitted that such a result suggests, even perhaps of itself requires, the supposition of some hidden aid which rectified the disproportion, and placed the means in a due relation to the end. Now, among the Hebrews of the period there is no sign as yet of intellectual predominance or advancement; and that such a man as Moses should have been raised up amongst them is a fact which of itself suggests and sustains the idea of some altogether special and peculiar guidance exercised by the Almighty over the selected people.

I cannot but think that, wherever we turn, we seem to find the broad and lucid principles of historic likelihood asserting themselves in favor of the substance of the Legislative Books, apart from questions of detail and literary form.

In its great stages, we are entitled to treat the matter of the narrative books as history entitled to credit. An elaborate organization, with a visible head and an hereditary succession, is, after a long lapse of time, substituted for a regimen over Israel, of which the mainsprings had been personal eminence and moral force. It is represented in the Scripture, and it seems obvious, that the transition from this patriarchal republicanism to monarchy was in the nature of a religious retrogression. It showed an increasing incapacity to walk by faith, and a craving for an object of sight, as a substitute for the Divine Majesty apprehended by spiritual insight, and habitually conceived of by the people as the head of the civil community. This view of the relative condition of republican and of regal Israel is confirmed by the fact, on which I have already observed, that with the monarchy came in another regular organization, that of the schools of the prophets. Prophecy, which for the present purpose we may consider as preaching, instead of appearing from time to time as occasion required, became a system, with provision for perpetual succession. That is to say, the people could not be kept up to the primitive, or even the necessary, level in belief and life, without the provision of more elaborate and direct means of instruction, exhortation, and reproof, than had at first been requisite.

Notwithstanding the existence of those means, and the singular and noble energy of the prophets, the proofs of the decline are not less abundant than painful, in the wickedness of most of the sovereigns, and in the almost wholesale and too constant lapse of the Israelites into the filthy idolatry which was rooted in the country. And again, it is not a little remarkable that the enumeration by name of the great historic heroes of faith, in the Epistle to the Hebrews, ends in the person of King David,* with the first youth of the monarchy. The only later instances referred to are the prophets, named as a class, who stood apart and alone, and were not as a rule leaders of the people, but rather witnesses in sackcloth against their iniquities. Taking the history from the Exodus to the Exile as a whole, the latter end was worse than the beginning, the cup of iniquity was full; it had been filled by a gradual process: and one of the marks of that process was a lowering of the method, in which the chosen people were governed; it became more human and less divine.

Under these circumstances, does it not appear like a paradox, and even a rather wanton paradox, to refer the production of those sacred Mosaic Books, which consti-

* Heb. xi. 32.

tuted the charter, and formed the character, of the Hebrews as a separate and peculiar people, to the epochs of a lowered and decaying spiritual life? They surely formed the base on which the entire structure rested. It is hardly possible to separate the fabric from its foundation. Had they not been recorded and transmitted, it would have been reasonable, perhaps necessary, for us to presume their existence. They could only spring from a plant full of vigorous life, not from one comparatively sickly and exhausted.

Again, we are taught by the negative school that the portion of the Pentateuch, which specially describes the work of the Priest, and which they term the Priest-Code, is of late composition, probably the latest of all, and has been devised in the interest of the priestly order.

Now I think that there are ready means of applying the touchstone to this allegation. It seems the great aim of the assailants to bring down the date of the main contents of the Legislative Books to the Exile and the period which follows it. Now we have to remember that the schools of the prophets established a caste which was in professional rivalry with the priesthood, and which presented every likelihood of being its effective censor. We have the written and, I believe, unquestioned productions of this school of prophets, reaching back into the ninth century (in the Book of Amos), above two hundred years before the Exile. The relation of the prophet to the priest, somewhat accentuated so to speak by competing interests, was in certain respects one of superiority; for, while the priest only administered in a human way a system originally of Divine appointment, the prophet believed himself to speak under direct inspiration and command from the Most High. The supposition pressed upon us is that, during the period when the Books of the Prophets were being produced, the priests foisted upon the nation adulterated, nay, rather forged, works, which they audaciously ascribed to Moses, and which they shaped in the interests of the sacerdotal order. Is it not quite plain that, if this had been true, nay, if it had been so much as an approach to the truth, the prophets would, in the interests of righteousness even more than in their own, have made use of the advantages of their position, and would have held up such a flagrant iniquity of the rival class to infamy or rebuke? Yet they do nothing of the sort. And it is not even open to us to refer this to some hidden cause, as it would have been if we could have alleged that, for some undeclared reason, it is their habit to pass by the conduct of the priests in silence. For, on the contrary, they do exercise the office of reprimand most freely. They do reprove and denounce neglect of duty and abuse of power by the priests; but they do this exactly in the same way for the priestly order and for their own; and, though they could not have been biassed against their own schools, there is no sign that priests were more faulty than prophets. By way of specimen of their usual manner, I may quote the prophet Zephaniah, who in the following passage appears to administer justice impartially all round:

"Her princes within her are roaring lions; her judges are evening wolves; they gnaw not the bones till the morrow.

"Her prophets are light and treacherous persons: her priests have polluted the sanctuary, they have done violence to the law." *

All were human, all were alike. There is nowhere a tittle of evidence to show the gross and very special offences with which the priesthood are now charged. In such a case the negative evidence carries positive force. It is evident, first, that the prophets knew nothing of such delinquencies: and

* Zeph. iii. 3, 4.

secondly, that, if they were unknown to the prophets through this long lapse of time, it was because they were not committed.

We have, then, in the historic Moses a great and powerful genius, an organizing and constructing mind. Degenerate ages cannot equip and furnish forth illustrious founders, only at the most the names and shadows of them. Moses belongs to the class of nation-makers; to a class of men, who have a place by themselves in the history of politics, and who are among the rarest of the great phenomena of our race. And he stands in historic harmony with his work. But we are now sometimes asked to sever the work from the worker, and to refer it to some doubtful and nameless person; whereas it is surely obvious or probable that the author of a work so wonderful and so far beyond example, so elaborate in its essential structure, and so designed for public use, could hardly fail to associate his name with it as if written upon a rock, and with a pen of iron. For, be it recollected, that name was the seal and stamp of the work itself. According to its own testimony he was the *apostolos*,* the messenger, who brought it from God, and gave it to the people. If the use of his name was a fiction, it was one of those fictions which

---
* Exod. xix. 16–25, and *passim*.

are falsehoods; for it altered essentially the character of the writings to which it was attached.

Supposing it to be granted that this or that portion of the Legislative Books may have been an addition in the way of development, of an appendage and supplement to a scheme already existing, how and why came it to be placed under the shelter of the great name of Moses, but because that name had already acquired and consolidated its authority, from its being inseparably attached to the original gift of the law?

Even so it was that, when the great and wonderful poems known as the Iliad and Odyssey had given to the name of Homer a surpassing celebrity, and other works of less exalted rank sought for fame by claiming him as their author, the simple fact that they so claimed him of itself supplied the proof that Homer was traditionally, and from immemorial time, taken to be the author of those greater works at the time when the lesser ones were imputed to him. If the title of Mosaic authorship was ever in any case attached to what Moses did not produce, the ascription was made in order to gain credit for the new supplemental matter, and of itself proved that, at the date when it was made, there was an older and immemorial belief in his being the author of the work whereto the supplement was appended.

As we stand on historical ground in assuming that Moses was a great man, and a powerful agent in the Hebrew history, so we stand on a like basis in pointing to the fact that, from the Captivity onwards (I say nothing of the prior period, as it would beg the question), the Jewish nation paid to the Five Books of the Pentateuch a special and extraordinary regard, even beyond the rest of their sacred books. These were known as the Torah; and the fact of this special reverence is one so generally acknowledged, that it may without discussion be safely assumed as a point of departure.

Before, then, any sort of acceptance or acquiescence is accorded to notions which virtually consign to insignificance the most ancient of our Sacred Books, let us well weigh the fact that the devout regard of the Hebrews for the Torah took the form, at or very soon after the Exile, of an extreme vigilance on behalf of these particular Books as distinct from all others. This vigilance, which at a later epoch reached its climax under the Massoretes, very naturally began, or greatly advanced, at the time when the nation, or its leading classes, having for the time lost their temple and their visible home, clung more closely than ever to the written word in their Sacred Books; to its body either more, or not less, than to its spirit.

So early as in the days of Hezekiah, there is said to have been a restorative process of some kind performed upon the text of the law, as well as upon the temple and its doors.* That clinging affection to the Word, which the Captivity could not fail to stimulate in pious minds, took effect, after the Return, in the establishment of positive institutions for its care; which, indeed, had become a necessity, in consequence of the change in the spoken language, unless it were to be wholly lost to the people. Hence we have the Jewish tradition of a Great Synagogue, founded with this view. A guild of scribes was appointed to copy, preserve, and expound the Divine Word,† and the Canon of the Old Testament appears during the same period to have assumed something of a regular form. Soon grew up the Massorah, or body of traditions concerning the texts of the Torah, which is supposed to have become noticeable from about 300 B. C.,‡ and which in after ages gave a name to the Massoretes, official students and guardians of the text. This body is

---

* Paterson Smyth, "The Old Documents," p. 42. 2 Chron. xxix. 3.
† Paterson Smyth, p. 66.   ‡ *Ibid.* p. 90.

one without a parallel in the history of the world. Its existence not only afforded strong securities of a special nature for the faithful custody of the text from the date when its operations commenced, but it also bears witness to a profound and exacting veneration for the Ancient Books as such, which seems to presuppose an unquestioning traditional belief in their antiquity and authenticity.

The Jews, perhaps exclusively among the early peoples, distinguished broadly between the matter and the corporeal form of a book, between its soul and its body. They alone conceived the idea of using the material form of the words and letters as an instrument for ensuring the conservation of the contents. If (such was their conception) we secure the absolute identity of the manuscripts, and reckon up the actual numbers of the words they contain, and of the letters which compose the words, then we shall render change in them impossible, and conservation certain. Thus, for example, the words in the Book of Psalms were counted, and the middle word of the book was known. The letters in each word were also counted, and the middle letter was known. Rules for writing, placing, and arranging were laid down; readings were noted as *khetibh* and *keri;* as what was in the text, and as what ought to be in the text but, from a reverent unwillingness to alter, only took its place upon the margin. The Hebrews were the only people who built up by degrees a regular scientific method of handling the material forms in which the substance of their Sacred Books was clothed, and this system had begun to grow from the time when a special reverence is known to have been concentrated upon the Torah. I will not dwell upon the topic that this peculiarity of handling supplies of itself a certain amount of presumption for peculiarity of origin. It may have commenced before the Captivity. It may have preceded, and may in that case probably have been enhanced by, the division of the kingdoms. It must have been in great force when, soon after the Captivity, schools of scribes were entrusted with the custody of the text of the law as a study apart from that of its meaning. Now, in our time, we are asked or tempted by the negative criticism to believe that all this reverence for the Books of the Pentateuch, having primarily the sense for its object, but so abounding and overflowing as to embrace even the corporeal vehicle, was felt towards a set of books not substantially genuine, but compounded and made up by operators, and these recent operators, who may be mildly called editors, but who were rather clandestine authors. Is this a probable or reasonable hypothesis? Is it even possible that these books of recent concoction, standing by the side of some among the prophetical books possessing a much greater antiquity, should nevertheless have attracted to themselves, and have permanently retained, an exceptional and superlative veneration, much exceeding that paid to the oldest among the Books of the Prophets, and such as surely presumes a belief in the remoteness of their date, the genuineness of their character, and their title to stand as the base, both doctrinal and historic, of the entire Hebrew system?

The result of this negative criticism ought to be viewed in its extreme form, and this for several reasons: such as, that, with the lapse of time, it continually adopts new negations; that the more conservative of the latest schools exhibit to us no principle, which separates them in the mass from the bolder disintegration; and that what is now the *ultima thule* of the system may, a short time hence, appear only to have been a stage on the way to positions as yet undreamt of. So viewing the subject, do we not find that it comes to this: not merely that the Mosaic laws received secondary supplements or amendments from time to time, but that the entire fabric had grown up anonymously as well as recently, and that it rests upon no guarantee whatever, either of time, or of place, or of personal authority?

I have already endeavored to show the historic improbability that an upstart production could have leaped into an estimation such as belongs to a firm tradition and a general credit of antiquity. And now let us look for a moment at the rather crude and irregular form of the Mosaic Books from Exodus to Deuteronomy. Taken as a whole, they have not that kind of consistency which belongs to consecutiveness of the parts, and which almost uniformly marks both historical and legal documents.* They mix narrative and legislation: they pass from one to the other without any obvious reason. They repeat themselves

* "As to this want of order (which seems to me to favor the idea of contemporaneity), a later codifier would have been more artificial in his arrangement" (Milman's "History of the Jews," 3rd Edition, 1863). Writing of the delivery of the law, the learned and very liberal-minded Dean Milman had before him the works of the critical school down to Bleek; and in the admirable note (i. 131) from which I have just quoted a few words, he expresses a firm and reasoned dissent from the negative conclusions as to the Pentateuch in its substance, while he strongly urges the likelihood of minor changes in the text with anachronism and inaccuracy here and there as the consequence. This note is in effect a succinct but highly pregnant treatise, and will well repay those who carefully peruse it.

in a manner which seems to exclude the idea that they had undergone the careful and reflected reviews, the comparison of part with part, which is generally bestowed upon works of great importance, completed with comparative leisure, and intended for the guidance not only of an individual but of a people. They are even accused of contradiction. They appear to omit adjustments, necessary in the light of the subsequent history: such, for instance, as we might desire between the sweeping proscription not only of image worship, but of images or shapen corporeal forms, in the Second Commandment, and the use actually made of them in the temple, and in the singular case of the serpent destroyed by Hezekiah.* It seems not difficult to account for this roughness and crudeness of authorship in the case of Moses, under the circumstances of changeful nomad life, and the constant pressure of anxious executive or judicial functions, combined with the effort of constructing a weighty legislative code, which required a totally different attitude of mind. The life of Moses, as it stands in the sacred text, must have been habitually a life of extraordinary, unintermitted strain, and one without remission of that strain even during its closing period. As some

* 2 Kings xviii. 4.

anomalies in the composition of the Koran may be referable to the circumstances of the life of Mahomet,* so we may apply a like idea to the configuration of the Legislative Books. It is not difficult to refer the anomalies of such authorship to the incidents of such a life, and to conceive that any changes, which have found their way into the text, may yet have been such as to leave unimpaired what may be called the originality, as well as the integrity, of its character. But how do these considerations hold, if we are to assume as our point of departure the hypothesis of the negative extremists? Under that supposition, the Legislative Books were principally not adjusted but composed, and this not only in a manner which totally falsifies their own solemn and often repeated declarations, but which supposes something like hallucination on the part of a people that could have

* See Rodwell's Preface to the Koran respecting the Suras. A critic in the *Magazine and Book Review* has cited against me the fourteenth chapter of Esdras ii., and the strange story it contains of the burning of the law and the rewriting of it by Ezra. This story dates at the earliest from the time of Cæsar, according to others from Domitian. Thus a tale which first appears five centuries after the alleged fact at once becomes authoritative, if it serves a purpose of negation. But even this story supports the argument in the text, for the law is continuously and miraculously reproduced by dictation to a body of five scribes.

accepted such novelties, and almost worshipped them, as ancient. In addition to all this, they assumed their existing shape, so wanting as to series and method, in a settled state of things, in an old historic land, with an unbounded freedom of manipulation, at any rate with no restraint imposed by respect for original form, and with every condition in favor of the final editors, which could favor the production of a thoroughly systematic and orderly work. Does it not seem that if the preparation and presentation of the Hebrew code took place at the time and in the way imposed on us by the doctrine of the thorough disintegrationist, then we stand entirely at a loss to account for the somewhat loose and irregular form of the work before us? And conversely do not the peculiarities of that form constitute an objection to the negative hypothesis, which it is an absolute necessity for its promoters to get rid of as best they can?

Let me again illustrate the case by referring to the Iliad. Those who have referred that work to a variety of authors, have been driven to very subtle and questionable arguments in order to exhibit some semblance of anomaly in the text, and have always been allowed to assume that the final editors under Pericles, or at whatever epoch, wrought with energy and purpose to weld the fragmentary material into a seemly whole. Is it conceivable that an operation such as we are now required to believe in could have been carried on without the sense of a similar necessity, or could so absolutely have failed in literary aim and effort?

I subjoin one further topic of the same class, as fit to be taken into view. The absence from the Legislative Books of all assertion of a future state, and of all motive derived from it with a view to conduct, has been already noticed. The probable reason of that absence from a code of laws framed by Moses under divine command or guidance, is a subject alike of interest and difficulty. It has sometimes occurred to me as possible that the close connection of the doctrine with public religion in the Egyptian system might have supplied a reason for its disconnection from the Mosaic laws * even as I suppose we might, from other features of those laws, draw proof or strong presumption that, among the purposes of the legislator, there was included a determination to draw a broad and deep line, or even trench of demarcation, between the foreign religions in the neighborhood and the relig-

* This topic is touched by Bishop Alexander in his Bampton Lectures.

H

ious system of the Hebrews. The connection established by Moses between conduct and earthly retribution or reward, must of itself have tended to depress, if not the idea of a future state, yet the expression of that idea in public documents. Especially we should remember that the work of Moses was national rather than theological.* His theology is a means of conserving the nationality, which was itself a forerunner and a means of preparation for the Advent. It is enough for my present purpose, that the absence of the doctrine of a future state from the work cannot be held to discredit the Mosaic authorship. But does not that absence help discredit the idea of a post-exilic authorship? Is it conceivable that Hebrews, proceeding to frame their Legislative Books, after the Captivity, and long after the Dispersion of the Ten Tribes, and after the light which these events had thrown upon the familiar ideas of a future life and an Underworld, as held both in the East and in Egypt, could have excluded all notice of it from their system of laws? We see something of this influence, in the noble passage on the dead, Wisdom iii. 1–8, to which there is no parallel in any of the pre-exilic books. If it was an influence impos-

---

* See Zincke, "Egypt of the Pharaohs and of the Khedive," p. 202.

sible to exclude at the later date, then the fact of the exclusion becomes another difficulty in the way of our accepting any such date concerning the substance of the Legislative Books.

It seems, then, that it is difficult to reconcile the results of the negative criticism on the Pentateuch with the known reverence of the Jews for their Torah, which appears absolutely to presuppose a tradition of immemorial age on its behalf, as a precondition of such universal and undoubting veneration. But if this be necessary in the case of the Jew, how much more peremptorily is it required by the Samaritan contribution to the present argument, and what light does that case throw upon the general question?

It seems certain that in mediæval times, and until the seventeenth century, Christendom knew nothing of a Samaritan testimony to the authenticity of the Mosaic Books, excepting from certain slight references in the works of the Fathers to "the ancient Hebrew according to the Samaritans." But, early in the seventeenth century, a traveller found, among the Samaritans of Damascus, a copy of the Pentateuch in the ancient Hebrew letters, and we are told that there are now about sixteen of these manuscripts in the various European libraries. The chief one in existence is guarded with sacred care at Nablous, the ancient Shechem, by a congregation still surviving of a few hundred Samaritans.* For questions of textual accuracy, this work is esteemed inferior to the Hebrew, though it is not wholly without a claim to more archaic forms.

The Samaritan Pentateuch is one of the most remarkable monuments of antiquity. Its testimony, of course, cannot be adduced to show that the Books following the Pentateuch have been clothed from a very ancient date with the reverence due to the Divine Word; indeed, it is even capable of being employed, in a limited measure, the other way. But as respects the Samaritan Pentateuch itself, how is it possible to conceive that it should have held as a Divine work the supreme place in the regard of the Samaritans, if, about or near the year 500 B. C.,† or, still more, if at the time of Manasseh the seceder‡ it had as matter of fact, been a recent compilation of their enemies the Jews? or if it had been regarded as anything less than a record of a great revelation from God, historically known, or at the least universally believed,

---

* See Paterson Smyth, p. 118.
† Paterson Smyth, p. 49.
‡ Placed by Wellhausen at about 375 B. C. "Hist. Israel," (Black), p. 498.

to have come down to them in the shape it then held from antiquity? Be it remembered that this work itself, and an approximate date for its known existence, are not matters of mere speculation, but are accepted results of historical research. And it is in this as in other cases a matter for serious consideration, whether we can accept the ingenious conclusions of critics before we know whether they are to be shattered and shivered when flung against the face of the strong rock of history.

The Samaritan Pentateuch, then, forms in itself a remarkable indication, nay, even a proof, that, at the date from which we know it to have been received, the Pentateuch was no novelty among the Jews. But may we not state the argument in broader terms? Surely the reverence of the Samaritans for the Torah could not have begun at this period; hardly could have had its first beginning at any period posterior to the schism. If these Books grew by gradual accretion, still that must have been an accretion gathering round the work within a single channel. A double process could not have been carried on in harmony. Nor can we easily suppose that, when the Ten tribes separated from the Two, they did not carry with them the law, on which their competing worship was to be founded. In effect, is there any rational supposition except that the kingdom of Israel had possessed at the time of Rehoboam some code corresponding in substance, in all except pure detail, with that which was subsequently written out in the famous manuscripts we now possess?

I have not attempted in these essays to discuss the general credit of the Historic Books; yet, in connection with the Samaritans, I must here touch briefly on a single point. The negative critics are fairly challenged to explain to us how it is that priestly fabricators, writing at a late date in the interest of their order, have so notably abstained from endeavors to glorify its virtues and honors, or to conceal its lapses from right. In a yet wider view we may ask how it has come about, that they have entirely avoided attempts to magnify the religious responsibilities of the schism which divided Israel. It seems indeed strange that if these Books were in substance framed after the Exile, and in times when a spirit of rigorous uniformity prevailed, a more emphatic and distinct censure should not have passed upon Jeroboam, on the simple ground of his having established a separate and rival worship.

The man of God, who came from Judah, did indeed testify against the altar in Bethel;

but that altar was associated with the golden calf established and worshipped there (as well as in Dan) by Jeroboam; and the testimony of the prophet, or man of God, against this altar, embraced " all the houses of the high places which are in the cities of Samaria," and was therefore a testimony against idolatry, not against mere schism.* The special sin of Jeroboam, which caused his house to be cut off, was not that he divided Israel, but that he degraded its religion by making priests of the lowest of the people.† Nay, the Books present to us the two illustrious prophets, Elijah and Elisha, as having Israel for their field, and as working there not on behalf of the Levitical priesthood, but on behalf of righteousness as against sin, and of God as against Baal; in complete conformity with the spirit of the prophetic Books, which so largely concern the ten tribes. How is it conceivable that men wicked enough to forge should so carefully have eschewed gathering any fruits from their forgery?

Let us close this portion of the subject with a plea of a different order, one which, admitting probable imperfection in the text, deprecates, as opposed to the principles of sound criticism, any conclusion therefrom adverse to its general fidelity. It has caused

* 1 Kings xii. 28, 29, 32; xiii. 32. † 1 Kings xiii. 33.

me some surprise to notice (1) that some negative writers lay considerable stress upon what they deem to be numerical errors in the Books of the Old Testament; and (2) that, so far as I have seen, they do not advert to the increased risks of mistake in the transmission of numbers as compared with other literary matter, whether it be by copying, or by word of mouth.

The increased risk, which accompanies all recording of numbers, extends likewise to enumerations, such as genealogical or other recitals of names in lists; subject, however, to the remark that, where metre is used, inasmuch as it supplies a framework for particular words which would not apply to other words, the danger is proportionably less; and also that, where the record is by writing and not by simple hearing, the eye has the opportunity of traversing again and again the names, as the mechanical process is carried on; and these names will in many cases stand in connection with, and so be seen to check, one another.

Bishop Colenso, for example, lays very great stress on the numbers assigned by the Old Testament to the children of Israel on their passage through the desert, and observing on the practical difficulties which such a multitude must encounter on a march treats the case as one which materially impugns the general credit of the history.*

I suppose that those who are practically conversant with the movement of men in large bodies may be much inclined to follow Colenso in questioning the statements of numbers, both at that point of their history, and in many other places of the narrative. It is quite another question whether, because errors may have crept into the numbers, the recitals of facts generally are therefore untrustworthy.

There is a broad and clear difference, of which note ought to be taken. Both in coyping and in original composition, as a general rule, the structure of the sentence, or what is called the context, is mentally carried onwards, and the general drift confines within narrow limits the possibility of error in the particular words. Mistake in the form would very commonly betray itself by inconsistency in the sense, and this inconsistency would not fail to be detected, because the relation between the parts of the sentence is ordinarily perceived as the process is carried on. But the relation between numerical amounts is not at once determined for the copyist by the context, and

* See Colenso on the Pentateuch and Joshua, part 1, ch. xii., *et alibi*.

usually requires a distinct and careful examination to detect it.

I will give two practical illustrations of this statement, the one very old and the other very modern; the one touching oral, and the other written transmission.

The most elaborate invocation of the Muse, or appeal for divine assistance, in the whole of the Poems of Homer, is the Preface* to the Catalogue of the Greek troops and ships; and this, although in no part of the poems could less of effort properly poetic be required. But the Catalogue consists partly of numerical statements of the strength of the contingents which made up the fleet, partly of geographical detail of the names of towns and districts; and here we find the rationale of the poet's call for special aid from heaven, and for his care with a view to accuracy, and this although he had metre to assist him.

I now turn to very modern practice. In the year 1853, it was my duty for the first time to submit to Parliament one of the large and complex statements of the public accounts for the year, which are associated in our country with the familiar name of the Budget. The speeches, in which these statements were contained, were made known to the country by reporting in the

* Il. ii. 484-93.

usual manner. But the art of the reporters could not be trusted to convey the figures with accuracy by the ear. A practice had consequently grown up of supplying them from the proper official source in carefully written statements for their guidance, which were sent to them during the delivery of the speech. It has now been found more convenient not to trust at all to the ear, and the Minister is understood to speak from printed figures: but this in no way weakens the illustration I have used.

My position amounts to but does not go beyond this, that the same care; which ensures general fidelity of statement in ordinary recitals of fact, does not suffice to secure numerical precision; and conversely that the want of such precision, which may sometimes be suspected in the Old Testament, does not raise presumptions adverse to general correctness.

The necessary limits of this essay do not permit of my entering on the contents of the Mosaic legislation. It is, I apprehend, both far more complex and far deeper than the other systems of ancient law known to us, as well as far higher in its moral aims. I humbly recommend that those who read it should fix their minds upon the skill with which it is addressed to the attainment of ends of such a nature as to render them, in their ordinary aspects, hardly reconcilable with one another. Severely proscriptive of the stranger, namely, the nations whom it found in possession of Canaan, it is as singularly liberal and generous towards him when he has made his peace with Hebrewism. Again, the Pentateuchal code differs from (I believe) all others in the extraordinary amount of its sanitary legislation, and in investing it with a quasi-moral character. But a sense of some strangeness in this respect alters into a profound admiration of the sagacity which includes in its far-reaching view provisions for giving an exceptionally high character even to the physical constitution of a people that was meant to remain socially separate from the nations of the world. Again: while aiming much at equality, simplicity, and industry, as fountains of order and of strength, it embodies most peculiar regulations for the purpose of restraining within the narrowest limits both that growth of wealth, which is their natural result; and also the spirit of enterprise, which would have burst prematurely the narrow bounds of Palestine, and destroyed the seclusion of the chosen people by untimely contact with the nations of the world. The design seemingly was to repress the latent powers of human nature, and to secure a conservative, even a stationary community, changeless as the truths of which it was the guardian. The completeness of the severance was not impaired by the Captivity and Dispersion of Israel, or by the Exile of the Jews in Babylon, or by the creation of Jewish factories abroad, or by the final destruction of the political independence of the country, or by the invasion and supremacy of the Greek language. The Jew, when our Lord came, was still, and was even more than ever, the Jew; and so, though it may have been despite of himself, the purpose of his great stewardship was accomplished.

On the Recent Corroborations of
Scripture from the Regions of
History and Natural
Science.

On the Recent Corroborations of Scripture from the Regions of History and Natural Science.

I. PRELIMINARY; II. AS TO THE CREATION STORY; III. AS TO THE FLOOD STORY; IV. AS TO THE GREAT DISPERSION; V. AS TO THE SINAITIC JOURNEY.

IT is to be observed, that many of the favorite subjects of scientific or systematic thought in the present day are of a nature powerfully tending to reinforce or illustrate the arguments available for the proof of religion, and for the authority of Scripture. If it had been actually proved, as it is largely argued and seriously held, that the vast and diversified scheme of organic life throughout the world has been evolved from a few simple types or possibly from one, such a demonstration would both enlarge and confirm the great argument of design. For this argument, instead of being drawn from particular and separate constructions, would then be drawn from the entire scheme of creation, and from the relation of all its parts to one another, inasmuch as every earlier portion of it would be an indication, and therefore a prediction, of all those which were to succeed; the seed of a long series of harvests to come. "Day unto day uttereth speech, and night unto night showeth knowledge." *

Again, the formal treatment in recent years of the subject of heredity not only tends to link the generations of mankind in one, but, in proving that our nature undergoes incessant modification through the influence of progenitors, enlarges our conception of the width of its range, and the varieties of those forms which it is capable of assuming. It shows us, for example, how the nature, as well as the environment, of descendants is deteriorated by the fault of ancestors, and how there may have been an education of the race from childhood to maturity, or some converse process of decay. Thus the doctrine of birth-sin, as it is sometimes called, is simply the recognition of the hereditary disorder and degeneracy of our natures; and, of all men, the evolutionist would find it most difficult

* Ps. xix. 2.

to establish a title to object to it in principle.

On these grounds, and on others more specific which it will be the aim of this essay to set forth in given instances, we should dispel wholly from our minds those spectral notions of antagonism between religion and science, which have been raised up by the action of prejudice on the one side, and perhaps by the occasional practice of bragging on the other. Of religion and of science, as of man and wife, let us boldly say, "What God hath joined, let not man put asunder." But I proceed to particular illustrations.

II.—AS TO THE CREATION STORY.

A double confirmation has, I conceive, in our time been supplied to the Creation Story of Genesis; the first by natural, and the second by historic science.

Perhaps we have been too readily satisfied with assuming, in regard to this narrative, a defensive position; whereas it may be found to contain within its own brief compass, when rightly considered, the guarantee of a Divine communication to man strictly corresponding with what in familiar speech is termed Revelation.

We have here in outline a primordial

history of the planet which we inhabit, and of the celestial system to which it belongs. Of the planet, and of the first appearance and early developments of life upon it, anterior to the creation of man, in many of the principal stages which have been ascertained by geology. Of the celestial organization to which our earth belongs, whether in all its vastness or only within the limits of the solar system we may be unable to say; but, at the least, a sketch of the formation of that system from a prior and unadjusted or chaotic state. Upon such a document a sharp issue is at once raised, at least as to the latter or strictly terrestrial part of it, the earth-history, for all those who hold it to be in its substance a true account. We accept from Science, as demonstrated, a series of geological conclusions. We have found the geology of Genesis to stand in such a relation to these conclusions, as could not have been exhibited in a record framed by faculties merely human, at any date to which the origin of the Creation Story can now reasonably be referred. Starting from this premise, we have no means of avoiding or holding back from the conclusion that the materials of the story could not have been had without preterhuman aid; and such preterhuman aid is what we term Divine Revelation.

And if the time shall ever come when astronomers shall be in a condition to apply to the earlier portion of the chapter the demonstrative methods, which geology has found for the latter part, it may happen that we shall owe a debt of the same kind, and of as great amount, to astronomy, as we now owe to geologic science. My present purpose is to call particular attention to the exact nature and extraordinary amount of that debt.

There was nothing necessarily unreasonable in accepting as worthy of belief this portion of the Book of Genesis, along with the rest of the Book, and with other books of Holy Scripture, on general proofs of their inspiration, if sufficient, apart from any independent buttress furnished either by science or by history for the Creation Story. In a court of justice, the evidence of a witness is to be accepted on matters within his cognizance, when it is consistent with itself, and when neither his character nor his intelligence are questioned; or again, when the main part of a continuous narrative is sufficiently verified, it may be right to accept the rest without separate verification. If, however, a new witness comes into court, and pretends to give us fresh and scientific proof of the Creation Story, this may be true or may be false. If false, the story is not disproved; it stands where it stood before. Bad arguments are often made for a good cause. But if true, the event is one of vast importance.

Now the present position is as follows. Apart altogether from faith, and from the general evidences of Revelation, a new witness has come into the court, in the shape of Natural Science. She builds up her system on the observation of facts, and upon inferences from them, which at length attain to a completeness and security such as, if not presenting us with a demonstration in the strictest sense, yet constrain us, as intelligent beings, to belief.

The Creation Story divides itself into the cosmological portion, occupying the first nineteen verses of the Chapter, and the geological portion, which is given in the last twelve. The former part has less, and the latter part has more, to do with the direct evidence of fact, and the stringency of the authority which the two may severally claim varies accordingly; but in both the narrative seems to demand, upon the evidence as it stands, rational assent. In regard to both, it is held on the affirmative side that the statements of Genesis have a certain relation both to the ascertained facts and to the best accepted reasonings; and that this relation is of such a nature as to require us, in the character of rational investigators, to acknowledge in the written record the presence of elements which must be referred to a superhuman origin. If this be so, then be it observed that natural science is now rendering a new and enormous service to the great cause of belief in the unseen; and is underpinning, so to speak, the structure of that divine revelation, which was contained in the Book of Genesis, by a new and solid pillar, built up, on a foundation of its own, from beneath.

It is, then, to be borne in mind that, as against those who by arbitrary or irrational interpretation, place Genesis and science at essential variance, our position is not one merely defensive. We are not mere reconcilers, as some call us, searching out expedients to escape a difficulty, to repel an assault. We seek to show, and we may claim to have shown, that the account recorded in the Creation Story for the instruction of all ages has been framed on the principles which, for such an account, reason recommends; and that, interpreted in this view, its entry into the argument is at this juncture like the arrival of a new auxiliary army in the field while the battle is in progress; like the arrival, to choose an historical instance, of the Prussians at Waterloo.

Such is the confirmatory argument

founded upon the contents. But now, yet another ally has come to join our ranks, under the title of Archæologic and Historic Science. It has deciphered the cuneiform inscriptions, and has read among them a Creation Story inscribed on the tablets found at Nineveh. Here we have a new witness to the very early existence, among civilized or partly civilized men, of records of creation corresponding in very essential particulars with the Hebrew narrative. Such a witness plainly to some extent offers to it confirmation; but also stands in competition with it. The competition is in those particulars where the accounts are not in harmony. As to these, standing on the character of its contents, the Hebrew tradition lays claim to superior antiquity and authority. But in proving the vast antiquity of certain fundamental ideas, the two are concurrent, and not competitive.

The Babylonian Creation Story is given by Mr. Smith in his "Assyrian Discoveries,"* so far as its mutilated state permits. It runs as follows, and we cannot, I think, but cherish the hope that it may hereafter receive extension or elucidation. " When the gods in their assembly made the universe, there was confusion, and the gods sent out the spirit of life. They then create the

* P. 397.

beast of the field, the animal of the field, and the reptile or the creeping thing of the field, and fix in them the spirit of life. Next comes the creation of domestic animals, and the creeping things of the city." Here we have, 1, creation by the gods; 2, chaos; 3, life, and only by inference, order; 4, wide extension of this life in beasts and reptiles; 5, after this the domesticated animals. Thus there is before us a real, though rude and imperfect, structural resemblance to the Hebrew narrative, together with the lowering interpolation of polytheism.

From the works of Schrader* on the cuneiform inscriptions, some further particulars may be gathered. He observes that in Berosus, as in Genesis, we begin with water and darkness. On which I would only observe that Berosus, who wrote in Greek, may not improbably have known the Mosaic writings,† and, as I have already stated, that water, in the text of Genesis, may be equivalent to fluid. The marked points of correspondence appear to be these : that the heavenly bodies are created after the heavens, which last expression, I presume, may be meant to include the light. That the land population

---

* Schrader, " The Cuneiform Inscriptions and the Old Testament." Translated by Whitehouse. Vol. i. pp. 4, seqq. † Smith, Biogr. Dict.

follows that of the water, and appears when vegetation has already begun. That the monuments name a Babylonian week, with the seventh day as a day of consecration, called also an evil day,* perhaps because evil for any work done on it. The inscription says:—

> " To redeem them, created mankind
> The merciful one, in whom is the power
> that summons to life."

which is faintly comparable with the words of Gen. ii. 7, and the Jehovistic account, " and breathed into his nostrils the breath of life." What seems to disappear from the Babylonian account is that evident intention of series and orderly development, or evolution, which is so wonderful a feature in the Mosaic narrative.

Dawson, in a recent work, observes that the polytheistic element is the distinctive feature of the Chaldean record, and that the originals of the tablets from Nineveh may have been very ancient, but that they are so mixed up with the history of the Chaldean hero, named Izdubar, as to suggest that there may have existed before it still older creation legends. He compares this record with the corresponding account in Genesis, which is as broadly marked with

* Schrader, p. 19.

the idea of the Divine unity as the Chaldean legend is pervaded by the conception of polytheism. And he adds, "Is it not likely that the simpler belief is older than the more complex; that which required no priests, ritual, or temple, older than that with which all these things were necessarily associated?" He naturally assigns a marked superiority to the "Hebrew Genesis."* In truth, that superiority seems to be not great only, but immeasurable. In one point only do the tablets go beyond the narrative of Genesis; they record the great struggle of Deity with rebellion, the war in heaven between Merodach and Tiamat. But, upon the whole, our Bible narrative is a regular structure; it is orderly, progressive, and rational; that of the tablets is dark and confused. This may, however, be referable in part to the imperfection of the tablets, the third of which, Mr. Sayce thinks, may probably have recounted the formation of the earth.† The one is charged in a marvellous way with instruction and moral purpose; from the other they have almost disappeared. The first has, as we believe, been receiving marked confirmation in the most vital particulars from cosmic and geologic science; on the second they can

* "Modern Science in Bible Lands," p. 32.
† "Hibbert Lectures," p. 394.

hardly be said to cast more than the faintest light. And yet this inferior document is itself of very great confirmatory value; for the Izdubar legends, says Mr. Smith,* appear to have been composed more than 2000 years B.C. There is no late date to which the Mosaic narrative can with a shadow of probability be referred. It could not have been formed without a miracle from the tablets as they stand. The two are evidently accounts proceeding from a common source, but derived through channels, partly or wholly independent. The one comes through a powerful and civilized empire, the other through an obscure nomad family. In the relative superiority of the Mosaic narrative, all the rules of merely human likelihoods are reversed; and the presumption of a Divine illumination is proportionably augmented. But the unsuspected antiquity of the inferior legend attests by an independent witness, if not the truth, yet at least the presumable origin, of its transcendent rival.

So far as scientific opinion is concerned, another remarkable confirmation seems to have been given to the cosmical portion of the Creation Story in Genesis by the course which it has taken of late years. Writing in 1839, Dr. Whewell devoted a chapter of

* "Assyrian Discoveries," p. 166.

his "Bridgewater Treatises on Astronomy and Physics"* to the Nebular or, as it is often called, Rotatory hypothesis. He described it in outline, as it had been conceived by Laplace. The idea of it was that the mass, which eventually centred in the sun, had revolved in a state of excessive heat; that, as it gradually cooled, the rapidity of its motion was increased; that, as the centrifugal force thus grew, the mass detached from itself exterior zones or rings of gas or vapor, which most commonly broke up into several minor masses, and so gradually formed the planetary system. Dr. Whewell's object in this early notice of a subject, which has since attracted, I believe, very general attention in the world of astronomical science, was to sustain and illustrate his general argument, by showing how this theory did nothing whatever to explain the origin of the system, or to weaken the statement of Newton, that its admirable arrangement must be "the work of an intelligent and most powerful being." The origin of this rotation, said Dr. Whewell, remains unexplained, and still as powerfully as ever cries aloud for, and proclaims an Author. My purpose in here naming the subject is to point out that Dr. Whewell then found himself dealing with a

* Ch. vii. p. 181.

theory which had not yet obtained any wide currency or authority, and he then "left to other persons and to future ages to decide upon the merits of the nebular hypothesis."* But, during the half century which has elapsed since he produced his Treatise, the hypothesis is understood to have gained very general, if not indeed unanimous, acceptance from astronomers. I refer to this result of the most modern studies as a new and remarkable establishment of accord between natural science on the one hand (so far as its reasonings have proceeded), and the Book of Genesis on the other. Often has it been endeavored to place the Mosaic geology in conflict with ascertained results, but less, though even here something, of the same kind has been attempted, so far as I know, by persons of scientific authority, with regard to the cosmogony which occupies the earlier portion of the Chapter. On the other hand, it has been shown, with what seems to me conclusive clearness, that, without the use of scientific language, that very process has been described in slight outline, but in singular correspondence with the hypothesis now so largely accepted. That hypothesis may not indeed have reached the point of demonstration, and this the subject-matter

* P. 190.

itself may be found not to permit; yet it has attained to so much of authority from consent that Dr. Whewell, were he writing now, would not have had simply to hand it over to the future for consideration, but would more probably have declared that it holds the field, and seems little likely to be displaced from it.

With the creation of the world or the solar system, the question of its termination is naturally associated. On this subject, however, I will not dwell at length, because the support here afforded by scientific opinion is given to the Scriptures of the New Testament, rather than the Old. To refer again to Dr. Whewell. In a passage of extraordinary grandeur, he delivered (I think it was in a sermon) his opinion that the world would end with a catastrophe, instead of dying what is termed a natural death. Such, as we know, is the emphatic declaration of the inspired Word. "The day of the Lord will come as a thief in the night: in the which the heavens shall pass away with a great noise, and the elements shall melt with fervent heat; the earth also, and the works that are therein shall be burned up."* And again, "Looking for and hasting unto the coming of the day of God, wherein the heavens being on fire

* 2 Peter iii. 10, 12.

shall be dissolved, and the elements shall melt with fervent heat." Such was the judgment of Dr. Whewell nearly half a century ago. His words were delivered rather as by one uttering his own firm opinion, than as expressing the conviction of astronomers at large. Nevertheless, as I have been informed on high authority, it is now the established conclusion of astronomers, based upon reasoning from ascertained facts, that the Galilean fishermen knew what all the genius and learning of the world for thousands of years failed to discover, and that—

> " The great globe itself,
> Yea, all which it inherit, shall dissolve." *

III.—AS TO THE FLOOD STORY.

I pass now to the Flood-Legend. one form of which has come down through Berosus and Josephus, but which acquires much more certain antiquity, and greater grandeur, from the Inscriptions. Their account, says Schrader, whose bias cannot, I think, be considered as friendly towards the Hebrew record, "brings the Biblical narrative into much closer relation with the Chaldean flood-legend than could be as-

* Shakespeare, *Tempest*, iv. 1.

sumed on the basis of the tradition in Berosus."* It forms part of the Izdubar legends discovered by Mr. George Smith, who published his account of them in 1872, and who assigns to them a date anterior to 2000 years B. C. under the early Babylonian empire.† The hero of the legends is believed by Mr. Smith to be the same as the Nimrod of Genesis. Like the Creation Story of Genesis,‡ that of the Flood derives corroboration from the Babylonian record, inasmuch as it is thus carried back by an independent testimony to a very great antiquity. That record, composed, as Mr. Smith thinks, not long after the time of Izdubar or Nimrod, gives us the tradition of a flood which was a Divine punishment for the wickedness of the world, and of a holy man, who built an ark, and escaped the general destruction.§ The particulars are set out in Mr. Smith's volume. They differ, in many respects, from those of Genesis, but the essential features are in the highest degree marked, and, together with certain of the details, are singularly accordant.‖ As in the case of the Creation Story, so here there is stamped upon them the note of a common source, and of channels of

---

* Schrader, as above, p. 47.
† "Assyrian Discoveries," p. 166.   ‡ *Ibid.* and 204.
§ Pp. 205–6, *seqq.*   ‖ Pp. 184, *seqq.*

I

descent which separate at some later date. In this case, however, the Babylonian narrative holds a higher position, relatively to the scriptural record, than in the case of the Creation.

The hero of the deluge is Hasisadra, a name which has been Hellenized into Xisuthrus; who, on the eleventh tablet, relates to Izdubar (the supposed Nimrod) the story of the deluge. I shall only attempt an outline presenting the main points.*

In the ancient city of Surippah, where Anu and other great gods were worshipped, Hasisadra was divinely warned by Hea, the great water-god, to construct a ship, of which the size is named, and commit to it "the seed of life, all of it," as "the sinner and life" were about to be destroyed by a flood. Food, furniture, wealth, servants, and animals were all to be embarked. The building and loading of the ship are then described, and the part taken by the several gods in bringing about the catastrophe. But "the gods" themselves feared the tempest, and "ascended to the heaven of Anu." This deluge lasted for six days: on the seventh all was quiet. There is sight of land from within the vessel. It is arrested by the mountain of Nizir. A dove is sent forth, and returns. A swallow is sent, and

* Smith, pp. 184-194.

does the like. A raven goes, feeds on the corpses that are afloat, and returns not. Then comes landing, sacrifice, the sending forth of animals. Ninip and Hea then remonstrate with Bel, and suggest other more usual means of chastising men, in which there seems to be some affinity to the promise of Gen. viii. 21–2, and ix. 11–17, that there should never again be a flood upon the earth. And "then dwelt Hasisadra in a remote place at the mouth of the rivers."

The resemblances between this narrative of the flood and that in Genesis are such as clearly to betoken a relationship at or near the source. The most peculiar, and at the same time purely incidental, among all the details of the narrative, appears to be the threefold experiment with birds upon the decline of the waters; but this appears alike in the three narratives of Chaldæa, the Bible, and Berosus. No other nations have accounts so full and precise as these.*

Mr. Smith has some judicious and impartial observations on the two accounts.† The Chaldean account indicates the nature of the country in which the flood took place. Surippah is near the mouth of the Euphrates, and there Hea was worshipped as the god of the deluge. The Hebrew account has no local confirmations of the story. When

* Smith, p. 212. † *Ibid.*

Surippah was conquered, in the sixteenth century B. C. or earlier, it is called in the record, "the city of the ark." Hasisadra is, like Noah, a devout man; and the Chaldean deluge is, like the Hebrew, a punishment for gross and widespread sin. Schrader argues with a view to attenuate this statement, but, as it appears to me, in the spirit of a partisan rather than a judge.* The dimensions of the ark vary in the three accounts; and on the variations of numerals I observe elsewhere. It may, however, be observed that the Babylonian account, which presumably was written down from a very early date, and in a durable form, has in this respect a great advantage over oral transmission, which is most of all dangerous for numerical statements. The inscription describes a regular vessel with boatmen, another incident of local color. The accounts curiously coincide in the minute point that, both inside and out, the ark is coated with bitumen. The tablet tells us that not eight only, but a comparatively large number of persons went on board. The Bible gives forty days as the duration of the flood, meaning apparently at the height. After 150 days the waters all abated. The whole duration before disappearance is a year and ten days.† The

* Vol. i. p. 49.   † Gen. vii. 11, 12, 13, 14, 17, 24.

tablet allows only seven days for the fulness of the flood. On the seventh day all storm has ceased. Hasisadra then sends out the bird. The ship is stranded for seven days more on the mountains of Nizir, so that the total term mentioned is one of only fourteen days. Nizir lies away to the east, far from the site of Ararat mentioned in Genesis; on the other hand,* the present tradition of the country lands the ark at a site farther to the north, and nearer Ararat. Again as to the birds. In Genesis Noah sends out a raven, which does not return; then a dove three times, at intervals of seven days; on the third occasion the dove does not return. The inscription sends, first, a dove, which returns, then a swallow, which returns, and then a raven, which does not return. Lastly, in the Bible, Noah lives after the flood for 350 years; the tablet and Berosus both assign to him, associated (rather strangely) with his daughter and the helmsman,† that translation to heaven for his piety, which Genesis gives to Enoch. Before translation, he was visited by Izdubar, and the region was deemed a sacred region.

On a general comparison of these two profoundly interesting records, the result appears to be that in what is circumstantial only there is much difference along with

* Smith, p. 217.   † Schrader, i. 60.

some curious resemblance; but in the outline of the fundamental facts, and in the moral considerations applicable, they are radically at one. The wickedness of the antediluvian world, the Divine anger, the command to build, the use of this vehicle of escape, and the erection of an altar of thanksgiving, are recorded alike in both. We have no absolute right to assume that either of the accounts, as it stands, is contemporary with the period of the flood. The points in which the Bible account may seem inferior, are the absence of local coloring, and the probable relation of the numerical statements to actual fact. Yet this, so far from impairing its claim to our acceptance, appears on the contrary to accredit it, because it is a feature which, given the circumstances of the case, there was reason to expect. If, indeed, we ride the hobby of the negative criticism, the Bible account bristles everywhere with difficulty. It is inconceivable that the framers should have in that case departed so widely from the inscription in points so palpable to all the world, or should have let slip the local color, with which a fabricator or late relator would have been forward to dress up his narrative. But, if we take Abraham, with his ancestors and his posterity, as a nomad people, religious and of simple life such as the Bible represents them; at an earlier period hanging on the outskirts of the Babylonian power, at a later one migratory towards the West; it was natural for them to drop the local coloring of a region with which all their relations had come to an end, and to drop somewhat behind in the exactitude of some among the particulars; and this is perhaps observable, as to the point of local color, not in the case of the flood only, but throughout the Abrahamic narrative down to the entry into the promised land.

The most significant difference of all between the two records is that the inscription is based upon polytheism, while in the Bible, here as elsewhere, all is based upon the doctrine of one God. That is to say, the simpler form is the groundwork of the Bible narrative, and the simpler form, according to the generally recognized principle, is that nearest the source, most closely akin to the occurrence or the original record. The religion of Noah agrees with that of the common father, Adam; the religion of Hasisadra has departed from the primitive belief, and exhibits to us those multiplied and deteriorated images of the Deity, which human infirmity and sin had introduced or allowed.

While Schrader glances at the period

when the Babylonian flood-legend reached the Hebrews as that of "the prophetic narrator of early Biblical history," he candidly adds, "I am led to the obvious conclusion that the Hebrews were acquainted with this legend at a much earlier period, and that it is far from impossible that they acquired a knowledge of these and the other primitive myths now under investigation as far back as in the time of their earlier settlements in Babylonia, and that they carried these stories with them from Ur of the Chaldees." For him they are all myths; the original invention is in Babylonia, and the Hebrews are early copyists. For others, however, they are in the nature of primitive traditions, founded on histories; and the twin versions bear testimony by their concurrence, and even in some respects by their discrepancies, to their historical character. If there was remoulding, it may be the more detailed and circumstantial narration which is presumptively entitled to the credit of it; and the Bible story, more sparing in its details, but far broader and more direct in the terrible lesson it conveys, may reasonably be judged to have come down from the source with the smallest amount of variation in essentials from the original. It is here as elsewhere. "The wisdom of this world," the race favored with stable institutions, and with intellectual development, yet fails in the firmness of its hold, and the clearness of its view, where the appreciation of the tremendous moral lesson is concerned; while the race of wandering shepherds, who are but the "babes and sucklings" of intelligence, yet transmit that lesson in a type so fresh and clear that our Lord has only to quote and enlarge without correcting it, and so to launch it anew into the world as a solemn chapter of His gospel teaching.

It may be noticed that the translation to heaven of Hasisadra, the Noah of the tablets, is in curious accordance with that far larger development both of the Underworld and of the future state, which marks alike the Babylonian and the Egyptian systems in comparison with that of the Old Testament, and forms an interesting but separate subject of discussion.

The Hebrew story of the Deluge has long been supported by a diversity of traditions among nations and races of the world, but never before with such particularity, or such corroboration in the sense and to the extent before described. But though we have now a new and important witness in court on our behalf, yet undoubtedly, if the narrative be provably untrue the testimony of both, or of any number of traditional witnesses, must fall to the ground.

The voice of natural science has not been, and probably is not at present, uniform on this subject. The negative has just been presented to the world, of course with great ability, and also in a sufficiently magisterial form, by Professor Huxley. He conceives that Christian theology must stand or fall with the historical trustworthiness of the Jewish Scriptures;* and, as these are not trustworthy, the consequence is that it must not stand but fall. With this general proposition I have here nothing to do.

Mr. Huxley selects the flood-story for the capital article of his indictment. But he treats it as little worthy of serious notice. "It is difficult to persuade serious scientific inquirers to occupy themselves in any way with the Noachian deluge." † He finds, indeed, a sort of historic nucleus for a partial deluge in the occasional desolating floods of the Euphrates and Tigris.‡ But, be it a partial or be it a general flood, he applies the same contemptuous negative doctrine to the deluge: perhaps most of all to what he terms a particularly absurd attempt at reconciliation, which places it "at the end of the glacial epoch." § I am far from

* *Nineteenth Century*, July, 1890, p. 8.
† P. 12.   ‡ P. 14.   § P. 13.

intending to enter upon a controversy, which I have no capacity to handle. Yet I may be bold enough to mention, that, while Mr. Huxley is speaking in the name of science at large, some votaries of science hold an entirely different language. Moreover, that the idea of a flood was not thus summarily dismissed by the luminaries of the scientific world anterior to the present day; and that the grounds of this dismissal are not of recent discovery, but were fully open to the geologists of the last generation. Quite recently, the doctrine of a deluge has been maintained by Sir J. Dawson,* by Mr. Howorth, and by the Duke of Argyll (if I interpret him aright),† all of whom are, I suppose, to be considered as "serious scientific inquirers."

Mr. Howorth, in his learned and laborious work on "The Mammoth and the Flood," is certainly not bound by any superstitious reverence for the mere text of the Book of Genesis; for, in his preface,‡ he seems to cast aside as null its traditions respecting all that preceded the creation of man. His treatise collects largely not only the diluvial traditions of so many races and countries, but an immense mass of palæontological

* "Modern Science in Bible Lands," p. 252.
† In *The Scottish Geographical Magazine*, April 1890.
‡ Pp. ix., x.

evidence; and, having laid this wide ground for his induction, he declares that, in his judgment, the whole points unmistakably

"To a widespread calamity, involving a flood on a great scale. I do not see how the historian, the archæologist, and the palæontologist can avoid making this conclusion in future a prime factor in their discussions, and I venture to think that before long it will be accepted as unanswerable." *

Moreover, I am free to consider history no less a science, though a less determinate science, than geology or biology; and I quote in conclusion the following passage from Lenormant, which follows a copious collection of testimonies to the tradition of a deluge in almost all lands:—

"La longue revue, a laquelle nous venons de nous livrer, nous permit d'affirmer que le récit du deluge est une tradition universelle dans tous les rameaux de l'humanité, a l'exception toutefois de la race noire. Mais un souvenir partout, aussi précis et aussi concordant, ne saurait être celui d'un mythe inventé a plaisir; aucun mythe religieux ou cosmogonique ne présente ce caractère d'universalité. C'est necessairement le souvenir d'un evènement réel et terrible, qui frappa assez puissamment l'imagination des ancêtres de notre espèce pour n'être jamais oublié de leurs descendants. Ce cataclysme se produit près du berceaux primitif de l'humanité." †

* P. 463.
† "Les Origines de l'Histoire," pp. 489,490. Second Edition 1880. "The long review, to which we have just applied ourselves, warrants our affirming that the tale of the Deluge is an universal tradition among all

IV.—AS TO THE GREAT DISPERSION.

The contents of the Tenth chapter of Genesis constitute a document of a character altogether extraordinary: for example, in the two following particulars. First, it is without parallel in the world. Nowhere else is there known to us a distinct and detailed endeavor to draw downwards from a single source the multiplication of men in the earth by families, and the distribution of them over the face of the earth. Secondly, this account, containing seventy-two names of men (to which more are added in connection with the descent of Abram when we reach chap. xii.), is so particular, that the notion of its correct transmission by ordinary means may appear to present much difficulty. Abram, when he migrated westward, came from a country which we now know to have possessed in his time means of durable record; but, as the head of a nomad family, he could hardly have carried

the branches of the human family; excepting, however, the blacks. But a remembrance prevailing everywhere, so precise and so concordant, cannot belong to a myth arbitrarily invented. No religious or cosmogonic myth presents such a character of universality. It must of necessity be a recollection of a great and terrible occurrence, which impressed the imagination of the ancestors of our race so powerfully as never to have been forgotten by their descendants. That cataclysm took place at a spot near the primeval cradle of humanity."

with him written traditions: and a specific narrative of this kind, like the Greek Catalogue in the "Iliad," presented great difficulties in the way of oral transmission through several, perhaps many, generations, down to the time when we may reasonably suppose the children of Israel to have acquired the art of writing during their sojourn in Egypt. The assisting Providence of God may suggest itself to the believing mind as having supplied the needful measure of that aid, which Homer* besought, in a kindred case, from the Muses. But the document, if thus considered, lays a certain weight upon our faculty of belief, and even offers a tempting invitation to assault from those who are adversely minded. This weight, however, is converted at once into a prop, into a buttress which well and stoutly supports the wall, when we find that this singular and, so to speak, exposed tradition has received in the most fundamental and vital points, from the researches of philological and of historical science, striking and, we may suppose, conclusive confirmation.

The foundation of the arrangement is the threefold division of the human race from a certain period of its history. If such a division actually took place, we might expect

---

* Il. ii. 484.

to find the traces of it in a threefold division of language, which has an unquestionable relation to race; and, conversely, such a divarication in language proves an early distribution of races or families, from which it took its origin. Without entering into details, it may be observed that the Book of Genesis associates the first distinctions of language with the local dispersion of man; and it is now known that, in days antecedent to the permanent bond of literature, such an association is agreeable not only to probability, but to the ascertained laws of experience. And now we find that comparative philology, dealing at large with the languages of the world, has resolved them into that very threefold division, which the distribution of man according to Gen. x. into three great branches anticipates and requires. Here is again an important service, rendered by modern science to belief.

It is true that the Bible (Gen. xi. 1) speaks of language as originally one, and that this proposition has not yet been generally affirmed by philology. Yet the way to it has been opened, and it need excite no surprise should the goal be soon attained. Professor Max Müller, I believe, says there is no proof that the Aryan, Semitic, and Turanian families of language had independent beginnings; that radicals existing in all the three can be traced to the common source, and that even the grammars may have been originally one. But this subject still awaits its scientific elucidation or decision.

The Table of Peoples presents on its surface some apparent anomalies; of which, however, a rational account can be given, and one which for the most part converts them into evidences in its favor. For instance, the Hamitic portion presents to us out of a total of thirty names no less than eighteen which are plural words, and which are therefore national or tribal, while only two of the same class are found in the rest of the account. But this seems upon consideration to illustrate what we know from history; namely, that the Hamitic races exhibited the most precocious development, and set up the earliest known civilizations of the world, those of Babylonia and of Egypt.

Again: the Cushite stock, after its regular order is arrested in ver. 7 of the chapter, jumps as it were down to Nimrod in 8–10. But we must bear in mind the greatness assigned to his individual position. He is the only person in the Table who is described as founding a kingdom, and the account of him has a great resemblance to that of Izdubar in the Assyrian Tablets, with whom he is identified by Mr. George Smith.

Again, as Shem, Ham, and Japheth are four times mentioned together, and invariably in this order, it seems to follow naturally that this is the order of their ages. In ch. x., however, their descendants are set out in the inverse order, and Japheth takes precedence. But this also, upon reflection, we may find to be quite natural. Migration was largely connected with considerations of space and food. It may be that the younger had to give place to the elder, and that the children of Japheth had on this account to be the first in moving from the common centre.

Further: in the Japhetic line the genealogy wholly stops with the next generation but one, whereas, it is continued farther, not only in the Semitic line, which had to be connected with Abram, but also in the Hamitic, by the mention of Nimrod and of the Philistines. This, however, seems perfectly natural if the line of Japheth, as is probable, moved the first, and, as is manifest, went the farthest, so as to be out of sight of the narrator, while descendants of Shem and Ham remained locally in contact with each other. Knobel* has observed, that in each of the three branches the enumeration begins with those who travelled to the greatest distance from the common centre

* "Völkertafel der Genesis," Giessen, 1850, p. 14.

(which is taken by him to be near Mount Ararat), and accordingly the Japhetites are reckoned from the north-west, the Semites from the south-east, and Hamites from the south-west. Just as in the case of the Homeric Catalogue,* this methodical arrangement probably gave great assistance to the memory of the first recorder.

Knobel has discussed with great minuteness and care the particular names of the recital, and he traces them to their historic seats. Bishop Browne, in the "Speaker's Commentary," has entered on the same field. Some examples may be given. The Japhetites are those (Japhah) of fair complexion. They take to the isles or coast-lands,† the seaward countries of the north and west. Here we meet the name of Gomer reproduced in the Cimmerians, Cimbri, and Cwmry. Ashkenaz, the son of Gomer, is found in Scandinavia,‡ the Scangia of Jornandus, the chief seat of the German stock. Another route is marked in the same direction by Ascania,§ in Asia Minor, a name found at various points of that region. Knobel thinks there is a trace of the Teutonic race in Teuthras, a name found on

* "Juventus Mundi," p. 467.
† See Revised Version, Gen. x. 5.
‡ Knobel, *Ibid.* pp. 35–7.   § P. 39.

both sides in the war of the Iliad.* He proceeds with the list of Japhetites as follows. Riphath, he thinks, is traced in the Carpathian country,† Togarma in Armenia, Magog in the Slavs, Madai in the Medes, Javan in the Iaones or Ionians, Elisa in Æolians, Tarshish in the Tursenoi, Kittim in the Chitians of Cyprus, Dodanim in the Dardanians, Tubal in the Iberians, Meshech in the Meschi or Moschi, Tiras in the Thracians (Thrax or Thras).‡ Some among these particular interpretations—for instance, that given to Elisa—may be untenable. Bishop Browne § sets out the various opinions that have been held, mostly without declaring a preference. It is not, however, the accuracy of each particular identification, nor even of every particular item of the text, but the principles of the general arrangement, and the large number of cases reasonably clear, which give the subject its importance.

The Semitic and Hamitic branches offer less difficulty to the investigator. No part of the tracking is more satisfactory than that which relates to the nations of Palestine, and to the names of Canaan, Sidon and Heth, where every particular, known to us from

* V. 705, and vi. 13.   † Knobel, *Ibid.* p. 44.
‡ Pp. 53, 60, 71, 77, 81, 95, 117, 123.
§ " Speaker's Comm.," Genesis *in loc.*

independent history or tradition, supports, so far as I can judge, in a most remarkable manner the trustworthiness of the record. Speaking generally, perhaps no one can go farther than Knobel in the work of identification. His treatise has become a considerable authority, and is of the greater value because he does not belong to the conservative school of criticism on the Old Testament.

V.—AS TO THE SINAITIC JOURNEY.

In his " Modern Science in Bible Lands," Sir J. Dawson has examined, with elaborate care, first the dwelling-place of the Israelites in Egypt, and their probable route from it until they cross the Yam Suph; and then, still more particularly, the account of their journeyings beyond the Red Sea. His conclusion is that they crossed at a point,* now forming part of the Bitter Lakes of the Isthmus, but then a part of the Red Sea itself, which was fed in ancient times by a branch of the Nile flowing eastwards.† Yam Suph, or sea of weeds, is the name given to it in the Bible.‡

Beyond the Red Sea, and onwards to the Sinaitic region, the country has been surveyed by officers of the British Ordnance.

* P. 389.   † P. 392.   ‡ P. 404.

All the instruments of modern science have been employed; the results have been published on a large scale; and the effect, as reported by Sir J. Dawson, has been "entire agreement of the members of the party on essential points";* and the ascertainment of such complete coincidence of the actual features of the country with the requirements of the Mosaic narrative, as to prove it to be a contemporary record of the events to which it relates.†

The route pursued by the Israelites down the coast of the Red Sea, and then to the eastward, was peculiar, as it seems to have been dictated by a combination of strategical considerations with those which concerned the subsistence of the people, and especially the supply of water. The local indications are on this account all the more remarkable. It is not possible, without exceeding the limits proper for the present observations, to convey the full force of the evidence which shows how the stamp of Egypt was impressed both upon the Israelites themselves, and upon the narrative in Exodus of their escape; inasmuch as it depends on the details of measurement, atmosphere, water-supply, and other physical circumstances, and upon their relation to the Mosaic narrative. The conclusions

* Pp. 371, 406   † P. 407.

reached have no direct bearing upon the proofs of a Divine revelation through the Scriptures, but they are of great historical importance in establishing the credit of the Book, and its contemporaneous character as to the substance of its contents.

Conclusion.

Conclusion.

IN closing this series of papers, it is right to record the admission that they can lay no claim to anything more than touching, and that but slightly, certain parts of a great subject. They omit many things important, perhaps some things essential. The essay on the Creation Story, indeed, aims at bringing out, in lieu of simple apology, what seems to me a distinct and specific argument in proof of a Divine Revelation. Except in that instance, their main design is to draw out, so far as they go, the force of that cumulative evidence witnessing to such a Revelation, which has been so wisely summed up by Bishop Butler;* and also to disembarrass belief in it from those difficulties which properly belong not to itself, but to exaggerations and excrescences against which it can carry no absolute guarantee. They form the testimony of an old man, in the closing period of his life.

* "Analogy," part ii. chap. vii.

It is rendered with no special qualification but possibly this one. Few persons of our British race have lived through a longer period of incessant argumentative contention, or have had a more diversified experience in trying to ascertain, for purposes immediately practical, the difference between tenable and untenable positions. Such experience is directly conversant with the nature of man and his varied relations; and I own my inclination to suppose that it is more germane to the treatment of subjects that lie directly between collective man and the Author of his being, more calculated to neutralize deficiencies, though not to impart capacity, than a familiarity with those material sciences which have supplied an arena for, perhaps, the most splendid triumphs of the century now far advanced in its decline. On this subject has been recorded the nobly candid admission of Mr. Darwin,* respecting the possible atrophy, through disuse, of the mental organs on which our higher tastes depend. Among those organs I cannot but include the organ of belief. On this subject, however, I am a biassed witness. It is for others to judge. I only offer a plea, not in proof of ability, but only in extenuation of defect.

There is in certain circles a very confi-

* "Life and Letters," vol. i. pp. 101, 102.

dent disposition to assert that, as regards belief in supernaturalism, the intellectual battle has been fought and won, and that victory is on the side of negation. It ought to be observed, before proceeding further, that supernaturalism is a term which includes the idea of God. A sense may be, indeed, loosely given to it, which confines it to the mode of His manifestations. But, essentially, if God be there, the supernatural is there; and the developments which proceed from that idea, even if they had been crushed and stamped out, might germinate again. It is not, then, a question of excrescences or of details; the life and essence of religion are at stake. It is the question of belief in what is not perhaps scientifically, but yet intelligibly, termed a personal God.

I shall presently enter on the moral causes which may have contributed, and even mainly contributed, to stimulate the negative tendencies of the day. I am now only endeavoring partially to test the justice of a Pæan, which is not warranted even by the established fact of a victory. The Pæan of the victor is the epitaph of the vanquished: and the victory, which is to warrant it, must be a victory belonging to that class of victories, which end the war.

That such a song of triumph is raised

there can be little doubt. It seems to have inspired the recent Articles of that very distinguished and not less upright writer, Professor Huxley, in the *Nineteenth Century*. But I have never seen a better example of the plenary satisfaction which possesses the mind of many among the negative athletes than in the following passage, taken from a writer of ability:

> "I set out from the standpoint that the mission of Freethought is no longer to batter down old faiths. That has been long ago effectively accomplished; and I, for one, am ready to put a railing round the ruins, that they may be preserved from desecration, and serve as a landmark! Indeed, I confess to having yawned over a recent vigorous indictment of Christianity." *

This purports to be a description of a certain state of facts.† Now, it is not the first time that we have heard description of the kind. Such a description was supplied in an earlier time by no less a person than Bishop Butler, who, I apprehend, was not among those given to exaggeration. His words are these: ‡

---

* Karl Pearson, "Ethics of Freethought," Preface, p. 5. The dramatic character of this declaration is brought to its climax by the fact that the work is dedicated to the members of King's College, Cambridge.

† It is far from being isolated. The same ideas are expressed with greater vehemence by Dr. Hardwicke, of Sheffield, in a preface to "Evolution," London, 1890.

‡ From the Advertisement to the "Analogy."

"It is come, I know not how, to be taken for granted by many persons that Christianity is not so much as a subject of inquiry; but that it is now at length discovered to be fictitious. And, accordingly, they treat it as if, in the present age, this were an agreed point among all people of discernment, and nothing remained but to set it up as a principal subject of mirth and ridicule; as it were by way of reprisals, for its having so long interrupted the pleasures of the world."

It seems pretty plain that at the time when the Bishop published the "Analogy" * a wave of unbelief was passing over the land. The spiritual declension of the Hanoverian period had set in ; and the standard of life, and of the ideas current concerning life, was sinking almost from day to day. The negative movement of the period may have been quite as vigorous, as widespread, and as self-confident, as that of which we now feel the pressure. Yet it dwindled, and almost disappeared ; and we may even say that, at the time of Johnson's social predominance it left hardly a trace behind.† Nor was this either the first or the last of

* In 1736.
† In 1797, when Wilberforce published his " Practical View," he spoke of "absolute unbelievers" as a class which he feared was an increasing one (chap. vii. sect. 3). Perhaps the great war of the years 1793–1815 tended to debilitate the religious mind of the country by drawing off mental force in another direction. I have, however, heard from persons of high authority, who were old when I was young, that the French Revolution generated a distinctly religious reaction on this side of the Channel.

the reverses which negation has suffered. At the time of the great Renascence of ancient learning in the fifteenth and sixteenth centuries, the cultivated mind of Europe sank far back into Paganism; but that ebb was succeeded by a flowing tide. Again, in my own earlier days, say in the second quarter of the present century, there was a great revival, both of the dogmatic sense and of the religious life in England; and the temper of the time, in the thinking world, was strongly adverse alike to worldliness, to indifference, and to unbelief. No man, perhaps, was better qualified to pass a judgment on this subject than the late Dr. Whewell; and he, writing in November 1853, and referring to an opinion expressed by a contemporary of smaller calibre than himself, says, "As to his assertion that scepticism is increasing, it is contrary to all my knowledge of the cultivated classes."* But as the third quarter proceeded, the sceptical movement set in with a wide and subtle power. History, then, seems to prove that these negative movements are subject not only to a hazard, but even to a law, of mutation; and that every one of them, when it has done its work, may cease to be. Of one thing we may be assured: such a movement derives no real strength, no true

* "Life of Whewell," p. 431.

promise of permanence, from an overweening self-assertion. The question is not what negation thinks of itself and of the opposing forces, but what is the intrinsic strength of the reasoning on which it rests.

I have said that, when it has done its work, it may cease to be. For doubtless it has a work to do. The wave that breaks and foams upon the rock exhibits to us not merely, as it might seem, a picture of violence and a source of danger, but a fraction of the vast oceanic movement, which is the indispensable condition of health and purity both to the water and the air, and to the populations by which they are respectively inhabited. If we believe in Providential government we might rationally believe, even where we did not see, that those boastful, and even powerful, agencies are not without their purposes prefigured, and bounded too, in the counsels of God. It seems, however, not difficult to discern a portion of those purposes; which may have been, first, to dispel the lethargy and stimulate the zeal of believers; and, secondly, to admonish their faith to keep terms with reason, by testing it at all its points; lest fancy, or pride, or indolence, or the intolerant spirit of sect or party, should have imported into their beliefs merely human elements that it may be very needful to eject.

While leaving to the champions of negation their title, whatever it may be, to insist on the utter blindness of belief, this at least I urge upon them: they ought to understand that it remains just as possible now as it was in the early or middle ages, to uphold belief in perfect good faith and with immovable conviction. In the advance of scientific knowledge, and of the critical art, I for one see much that corrects and chastens what was temporary or accidental in our persuasions concerning the subjects of belief, but nothing that disintegrates or undermines the basis of belief itself; much, on the contrary, that confirms it.

It is sometimes taken for granted or alleged, that religion or its champions are reduced to the necessity of defending their cause only with arms which have been superseded, either by the introduction of forces previously unknown, or by new forms of construction better adapted to their ends. In a spirit which seems to fluctuate between pity and a good-natured contempt, Professor Huxley describes "the old-fashioned artillery of the Churches," on the one side, and "the weapons of precision," used by the advancing forces of science on the other.* Now let it be remembered that we have not here to do with the masses of mankind, **to**

---

* *Nineteenth Century*, July 1890, p. 22.

whom historical and scientific arguments, whether negative or affirmative, are, and probably must remain, inaccessible. We are speaking of that standing army, so to call it, of more or less instructed persons, who, on the one side and the other, execute all the fighting on behalf of the community at large. Writing, then, of those within the palisades of the lists, and not appealing to mere numbers, I demur entirely to the statement of Professor Huxley. I deny that the weapons of belief are antiquated: I pause even before admitting that those of scientific men are always, except in their own particular sciences, weapons of precision. When we decline the appeal to the established facts of science, or to the conclusions upheld or reasonably sustained by human experience through history, or when we fall into the trap laid for us by Hume, and treat the acceptance of our "holy religion" as a matter in no way amenable to the view of reason; then we may be justly charged with the use of weapons never worthy, and no longer serviceable. But until then, we may quietly endeavor to proceed as rational beings upon rational considerations. If these principles have not uniformly guided me in the composition of the essays I am now bringing to a close (on which it is not for me to judge), at least I can say that

K

there has not been in any instance, even by a hair's-breadth, an intentional deviation from them.

The fact, however, of a strong and widespread negative movement among important and active sections of our countrymen during the latter portion of this century is admitted; and now I propose to offer some remarks upon its alleged or probable causes.

I shall speak, first, of the detriment which religion is supposed to have suffered through the great and wonderful advance both of science and of rational speculation, mostly physical, but also critical, archæological, and historical.

Secondly, of the detriment it has suffered through the exposure to the world of erroneous notions about religion, which are due to believers themselves: a detriment attending, in different manners and degrees, either the retention, or even the abandonment of these opinions. Such detriment seems to me certain to ensue, when we uplift into the region of dogmatic truth (for example) such propositions as the following.

1. That the material volume of the Holy Scriptures, translated into our tongue, with every fact and sentiment it contains, must be received under the same (so to call it) materialized conception, as that under which

Mahometans are supposed to receive the Koran, and held absolutely true ; or 2, that there is no progression or distinction in the inspiration to which it is to be referred ; or 3, that the Adam portrayed in Scripture was the exclusive source of the race ; or 4, that he was furnished with large intellectual development and endowment.

Thirdly, I shall speak of the strength which the negative movement has in my opinion derived from causes greatly and subtly effective, yet wholly extrinsic to itself; causes, which I take to constitute its principal strength.

Of the first head I might dispose very briefly. I have enumerated some of the great services which science has rendered, and is rendering, to religion. Of the damage it has inflicted I have heard much ; but the allegations commonly appear to me upon examination to be found untrue: in some cases, like that of the first Chapter of Genesis, to be not only untrue but contradictory of the truth, inasmuch as science, when just principles of interpretation are called in, is found to have established what it has been charged with destroying.

The nearest semblance, that has attracted my notice, to palpable contradiction between modern science and Holy Writ is upon the statement that sin brought death into the world, whereas we now know that death was antecedent to the introduction of man, and therefore of sin. But in Scripture, beyond all dispute, the word death has many senses. For example, it means habitually, severance of spirit from body. It means separation from God, and domination of body over spirit.* It means reunion with God, and domination of spirit over body. † As it means the soul's disease, severance from God, so also it means the final consummation of that disease in the second death. These are various senses of the term, dispersed about the Bible. How do we know that St. Paul used the words in the first of these and not in the second? And if he had used it in the first sense, and had intended to declare that there was no physical death before the sin of Adam, how much would this prove? Only that the apostle was ignorant of any pre-Adamite history of the planet, and that we should have to ask whether such ignorance, when proved, would destroy or impair the overflowing proofs that he was commissioned of God to speak, and was taught of God how to speak, for the salvation of the world?

It remains, however a vital portion of our duty, on the one hand, to estimate and to

---

* Luke i. 79; John viii. 51; Eph. ii. 1.
† Col. ii. 20; iii. 3; 2 Tim. ii. 11.

measure aright the differences between the Divine Revelation in itself, and the subjective conceptions entertained and propagated concerning it; and on the other to inquire pretty strictly whether the professors of science are sometimes apt to push their legitimate authority beyond their own bounds into provinces where it becomes an usurpation, and whether the weapons which they hurl, are then always "weapons of precision"?

On the first of these two points, I will give an illustration of my meaning from the latest writings of the Achilles of the opposing army. In a very recent article, which deals chiefly with the Deluge,* Mr. Huxley, in a succinct but decided way, administers capital punishment also to the Creation Story of Genesis. He does not enter much into particulars, but he says the Israelites were like all other men, curious to know their origin. Now, so far as the records of the past go, the cosmological curiosity of the ancients appears to have been comparatively small. The cosmologies of Babylon and Egypt hold an utterly insignificant place in their systems of knowledge. The Greeks, perhaps the most inquisitive of men, cared little or nothing for these things, through many centuries

* *Nineteenth Century*, July 1890, p. 21.

after they had felt the passion of high poetry and of the legends associated with it; and when their schools of philosophy arose, they dealt, and this only in outline, with the origin of material things, rather than of men. There was no nation, I believe, except the Israelites, whose cosmology held a classical place in their memory and in their devotions. But I am perhaps wrong in arguing the question. What I ought rather to point out is that while Professor Huxley is fond, as he well may be, of claiming to represent science, his *dictum* is entirely outside the sciences he represents.

Again, in the same short space he proceeds to lay it down that an opinion given by Dr. Riehm on the subject of the seven Mosaic days (*i. e.*, that they are natural days) should be final. We claim, however, to be, if not Freethinkers, yet free thinkers. Why are we to renounce the faculty of discourse, to square our minds to those of Dr. Riehm, to let him do the thinking for us, and to accept his words as "final"? Simply because Mr. Huxley has said so. What right has Professor Huxley to close this question? For the question whether the Creation Story of Genesis describes solar days or not, is no more a scientific question, than whether Parliament should or should not meet in November, or whether Shakespeare wrote or did not write the whole of "Henry the Eighth."

But I have now to ask whether the weapons used by this most distinguished scientist are always "weapons of precision"? On scientific grounds he condemns, as we have seen, the narrative of the Deluge, and pronounces it to be fabulous. One of his reasons is this. The Mosaic account assigns a period of one hundred and fifty days (the Tablets give only seven) for the subsidence of the waters. Against this statement Mr. Huxley advances a *dictum*, of which the subject-matter is unquestionably scientific. He gives the length of the Mesopotamian plain * at three to four hundred miles, and the elevation of the higher end at five to six hundred feet. Had this plain been so covered with water, says Mr. Huxley, a "furious torrent" would have rushed downwards, and instead of an hundred and fifty days the plain generally (this word no doubt is meant to except particular hollows of the ground) would have been left bare in a very few hours.

Let us try this question a little more nearly. If the length of the plain be 350 miles, and the fall 525 feet, we have a descent of one foot and a half per mile; and this descent, says the Professor, would cause a

* *Ibid.* p. 15.

furious torrent, such as would clear the plain in a very few hours. Let us assume twenty miles an hour as the rate of the "furious torrent"; on which assumption, the plain would be bare in seventeen and a half hours. I take these rates and figures so as to translate approximately into definite quantities Mr. Huxley's more general expressions.

One foot and a half per mile represents a gradient of $\frac{1}{3420}$. I have sought information on this subject from an engineer, who is in charge of a portion of one of our rivers. I understand from him that a fall of one in three thousand four hundred and twenty would probably produce a current of about two miles an hour. It may require all Professor Huxley's resources to show that a current of two miles an hour is a "furious torrent"; or that to represent as a furious torrent what is in truth an extremely slow stream is to use a "weapon of precision."

My informant, indeed, adds that each case has modifying circumstances of its own, and must be judged by itself; but he likewise tells me that if, instead of taking an ordinary English river we remove the banks, and suppose the stream indefinitely widened, the fall remaining the same, the rate of the current would be not increased but slackened. Thus we seem to get farther

and farther from the " weapons of precision."
And it seems just possible that, after all, these
weapons may, like our monster guns, sometimes damage those who handle them, or
may fail to batter down so soon as is expected the undoubtedly ancient walls of the
fortress of belief.*

The case to which I have last referred is
one of elementary hydraulics. The obligation to be precise may be thought to rise
with the elevation of the subject. If we
may not ask from the scientific man that
when he touches questions of the innermost
feelings of believers, and of the highest
destinies of man, he should be reverent, yet
surely we are entitled to require of him that
he should be circumspect; that he should
take reasonable care to include in his survey
of a case all elements which are obviously
essential to a right judgment upon it.

In another recent article,† Mr. Huxley
has touched very lofty ground indeed. He
selects as a crucial instance for the trial of
the Gospels, and with them of the character
of our Lord, the miracle which happened in
the country of the Gergesenes, or Gadarenes.
It is narrated, with certain variations, by

* It is not without interest to remark that, on the data before us, the time required for clearing the plain would be about 162 hours, or nearly seven days, the actual time mentioned in the Babylonian account.

† *Nineteenth Century*, Feb. 1889, pp. 171, 172.

three Evangelists; the essential point being, that evil spirits, cast out from the body of a demoniac, are permitted to enter into a herd of swine, and that the animals rush furiously into the sea. Mr. Huxley, as a physiologist, disbelieves in demoniacal possession, and that is the point that has commonly attracted the chief share of attention in connection with this miracle. Such a physiological judgment it is not for me to discuss. But he also very properly touches the question of the injury inflicted by the destruction of the swine, which was due to our Lord's permission. Mr. Huxley observes that the Evangelist has no "inkling of the legal and moral difficulties of the case," and adds, the devils entered into the swine "to the great loss and damage of the innocent Gerasene or Gadarene pig-owners." Further, "Everything that I know of law and justice convinces me that the wanton destruction of other people's property is a misdemeanor of evil example."

So then, after eighteen centuries of worship offered to our Lord by the most cultivated, the most developed, and the most progressive portion of the human race, it has been reserved to a scientific inquirer to discover that He was no better than a lawbreaker and an evil-doer. It is sometimes said that the greatest discoveries are the most simple. And this, if really a discovery, is the simplest of them all. So simple that he who runs may read, for it lies on the very surface of the page. The ordinary reader can only put the wondering question, how, in such a matter, came the honors of originality to be reserved to our time and to Professor Huxley?

Simple as it has been from his point of view, the case * is to a reflective mind a very peculiar one. It offers the only occasion on which our Lord exercised, or co-operated in the exercise, of preternatural power for the destruction of life.

It is observable that in certain instances, such as that of the fig-tree, and of the ass with her colt, He seems to assert Himself as the universal owner. He is the Lord to kill, as well as to make alive, according to His wisdom. But this consideration, to whatever conclusion it might lead, is of what may be termed an esoteric nature, and is hardly suited to an argument against the negative school, who are plainly entitled to raise the question of the swine as it affects the rights of property. Why, then, does our Lord in this instance see cause to vary from the philanthropic and beneficent tendencies, which usually mark His miraculous agency? It has been observed that the

* Matt. viii. 30; Mark v. 2; Luke viii. 31.

entrance into the swine may have been permitted, in order to certify the man or men relieved of the reality of the great and hardly credible deliverance vouchsafed to him. And again, that the willing departure of the demons may have spared the victim or victims from the tortures, which it is natural to suppose would have attended their violent ejection. Yet something more seems to be desirable in order to meet the question that has just been raised. I find the answer to it in the reasonable, and (as it seems to me) almost necessary supposition, that the possession of the swine was unlawful, and, therefore, was justly punishable by the ensuing loss.

The scene is described by different Evangelists in different terms. It is the country of the Gergesenes, or the country of the Gadarenes. The distinction is immaterial to the present purpose. It was apparently part of the land of the Girgashites,* one of the seven Canaanitish nations, and was subject, therefore, as a matter of religious obligation, to the Mosaic law. Now that law contained a prohibition to use various meats, among which pork was included. But in the case of swine the law went farther than in other cases, and it was forbidden even to to touch the carcass.† Such a prohibition

* Deut. vii. 1. † Lev. xi. 7, 8.

of course precluded all use whatever of the animals when dead; and it was only for use when dead that there could be any object in keeping them at all. Nor was this prohibition merely ceremonial. It was immediately related to the health of the people, as the use of pork (I am informed) produces the disease called trichinosis, and I understand that the veto is down to this day regarded by well-informed Jews as of a serious importance; and is directly connected with a high sanitary condition.

It may be that the deeper counsels of Providence are more implicated in this prohibition, than even a less superficial reader of the Gospels than Professor Huxley might at first sight suppose. That calling of the Hebrew people, which is set before us in the Old Testament, demanded in them above and beyond all other qualities the quality of persistence. It may be that this purpose required the constitution of the race in body as well as in many points of character to be raised to a point unusually high. We know that man is a compound being, and we know that the Mosaic code took cognizance of bodily health to an extent quite unknown in other schemes of legislation. In the Book of Exodus,* reference was made to the superior forma-

* Ch. i. 19.

tion of the Hebrew women for the great office of a mother, and I am informed that the modern researches of anatomists, supporting the text, refer the fact to a physical cause. I have learned enough from some high medical authorities to be warranted in saying that the sanitary qualities of the Jewish race, even in our own time, and their superior longevity, appear in no small manner to be due to the strict observance of the Mosaic law. These remarks may be justifiable in connection with what I have said of the description of authority, which they attach to a particular prohibition. Yet for the immediate purpose of the argument it may suffice to have pointed out the illegality of keeping swine.

Mr. Huxley, exercising his rapid judgment on the text, does not appear to have encumbered himself with the labor of inquiring what anybody else had known or said about it. He has thus missed a point which might have been set up in support of his accusation against our Lord. Some commentators have alleged the authority of Josephus for stating that Gadara was a city of Greeks rather than of Jews, from whence it might be inferred that to keep swine was innocent and lawful. This is not quite the place for a critical examination of the matter; but I have examined it, and have satisfied myself that Josephus gives no reason whatever to suppose that the population of Gadara, still less (if less may be) the population of the neighborhood, and least of all the swine-herding or lower * portion of that population, were other than Hebrews, bound by the Mosaic law. Now, this being the case, the punishment inflicted upon the owners of the swine by the permission of our Lord, did not constitute a breach, but rather a vindication of the law; as a law would be vindicated if casks of smuggled spirits were caught and broken open after landing, and their contents wasted on the ground.†

Surely if these were only possibilities, instead of rather cogent likelihoods, they should have been examined and weighed before pronouncing sentence on One who, apart from all other claims, must be supposed to have had some considerable reason for deviating from His usually beneficent and gentle methods. And, again, such hand-over-head reasoning is hard to reconcile

* It is clear that such people could not be the owners of 2000 swine. But (1) this is stated in St. Mark only; (2) it is stated in a parenthesis, whereas it would naturally appear in the direct narrative; (3) so large a number suggests the error of a copyist or very possibly a marginal gloss.

† For the further elucidation of this important case, I have added a note at the end.

either with the judicial temper, or with the claim, nay the exclusive claim, to the honor of using " weapons of precision."

There is yet another point of great importance, in regard to which I desire to challenge the methods pursued by some critics of the Holy Scriptures; and I cannot do better than again proceed on the recent article of Professor Huxley. He finds, on the one hand, a vast mass of diversified tradition, which agrees in reporting a Flood. He finds that, as we draw near to that central seat of civilization in Chaldæa, from which Abraham probably carried the Hebrew narrative, it unfolds largely into detail, and that the tradition, which thus emigrated, is supported in many very remarkable particulars by the history which has been recorded in the Tablets. Finding, however, in the Mosaic story various statements which he deems to be irreconcilable with natural laws, he protests, not against those particular statements, but against the entire relation; and he casts aside without more ado, not only the whole tale as it is given in Genesis, but the large mass of collateral testimony, from every quarter of the globe, which supports it. Is this a scientific, is it a philosophical, is it altogether a rational method of proceeding?

Errors, and even great errors, may creep

into a true narration. This is a case where the tale had, according to all appearances, been carried orally for ages, perhaps for very many ages, before the race that have transmitted it to us had the means of giving it a written form. Was it not likely that some, perhaps even that much, variation of particulars would creep in? Could they be shut out except by miracle, and has the Christian Church ever taught us to believe in such a miracle? Is it not the fact that, as between the Chaldee and the Hebrew reports, the essence of the story remains in absolute integrity? A divine warning, a woful prevalence of sin, a terrible inundation or deluge as a punishment, the rescue of a small and righteous remnant; not only do these things remain, but traditions supporting them in several or in all points have descended to us independently through a hundred channels; and we are now asked to believe that, in each of these, imagination, and imagination only, has been at work, and that in each of them it has worked with an essentially (though not circumstantially) identical result? May not this be to substitute for a great physical a greater moral miracle, and are we not even in some danger of exchanging the unaccountable for the absurd?

My conclusion, then, upon this part of the subject, be it worth much or little, is threefold. I am grateful to science, both physical and historical, for the noble services it has rendered to belief by the establishment of truths, or by the rational acceptance of propositions, in its own domain. I feel that science is not responsible for any errors of scientists, either in the misconstruction of the Bible, or in offences which their share of human frailty may have led them occasionally to commit against the known laws of rational discussion. And, lastly, I am grateful both to science and to scientists for having assisted, or for having compelled, those who believe to correct errors which, in the wantonness of power, they may too long have cherished, and to submit all their claims to free and critical investigation.

The retreat from an untenable to a tenable position is in itself an unmixed good. We feel that we have redressed a wrong which had been done to Truth; and we breathe the more freely for the act. Still there is a retribution in store for error; and, given all the conditions of human feeling, thought, and action, this recession is an operation of invariable danger, and, for the time at least, of mixed result. Happy they who accurately know, and who exactly realize to themselves, in the practical part of their being, what it is that they ought to abandon and what to retain, nor only to retain, but to uphold with a determination enhanced in proportion to the difficulties of the day. But in the minds of many, perhaps of the greater part, the dominant sense, at least for a time, will be that they have passed from a ground old and familiar to one new and strange; that they have parted with something, they do not quite know how much; that if they have been wrong once, they may, perhaps, be wrong again. And then it is so much easier to believe in a volume, which the hand could grasp, than to hold fast the mental conception of a Revelation conveyed in that volume. True, such a conception of God in the Bible, which may be, but ought not to have been, a new one, is strictly and solidly analogous to the familiar, and equally indispensable, conceptions of God in Nature, God in Providence, God in the Christian Church. But these we had from our cradles; they were thoroughly congenial through use. To apply the same rule to the Bible is really to integrate, rather than to disintegrate, the idea of our knowledge of God. But there is something like the discomfort of a new habiliment to be got over; and there are the ready, sometimes, perhaps, the too ready, taunts of the adversary to be endured.

I will not dwell at large upon other difficulties springing from errors or the incaution of believers; but they are grave in their nature. Whenever, under the idea of magnifying the grace or favor of God, we derogate from His immutable righteousness and justice; and whenever, in exalting the unspeakable mercy of His pardon, we unhinge its inseparable alliance with a profound and penetrating moral work in the creature pardoned: then we draw down dangers upon the Christian system greater far than can ever be entailed upon it by its enemies. But there may be worse still than this. Worse there will be, if the believer in Christ holds the doctrine without giving effect to it in his life; and worst of all, if while he holds it he not only is betrayed into the ordinary weaknesses or excesses of human nature, but forgets also, and derides or disregards those primal sanctions of natural morality, which vice itself is not always hardened enough to discard. The constitution of the family, the ties between its members, the nature of the woman and of the man, and the relation of each one of them to himself, to that SELF, which is entrusted by God to every one of us to study and to revere, as well as to cleanse, to cherish, and to sanctify; all these are regulated by laws the oldest, holiest, and most profound of all.

Progress may be traced and tested by its regard for these sacrosanct, though unwritten, ordinances. According as such regard is paid or not paid, we shall know whether such progress be a realty or an imposture; and Christianity itself would lose all its titles were it capable of an attempt to disturb them.

In the class of difficulties thus roughly suggested has been, as I believe, not, indeed, a legitimate, but a powerfully operative, cause for the increase of scepticism.

But the gravest portion of the case remains. Negation is in part, and it professes and believes itself to be altogether, an affair of the intellect. It proclaims, for example, that the reason why unbelief has (at the moment) so much advanced, is that dogmas like those of the Trinity, the Incarnation, the Sacraments, and the future judgment have become insufferable to the cultivated human understanding. The conviction which possesses my mind, and which I may find it difficult to express in an unexceptionable manner, is that the main operative cause, which has stimulated the growth of modern negation, is not intellectual but moral; and is to be found in the increased and increasing dominion of the things seen over the things unseen.*

* In a work of great ability just issued, and termed "Scientific Theology," Mr. Barber, a civil engineer,

Such a proposition may at first sight appear to carry an odious meaning, pharisaical in the worst sense of the word; a meaning which would provoke and might justify, an angry reply. It might be interpreted as implying that the elevation of moral character in individuals varied with and according to the amount of their dogmatic belief; a proposition which in my view is untrue, offensive, and even absurd. Had I ever been inclined to such a conception, the experience of my life would long ago have undeceived me. My meaning is a very different one. I speak of that which touches not this or that man only, but us all. We have altered the standard of wants; we have multiplied the demands of appetite; we have established a new state of social tradition, of that tradition which forms and guides us, apart from and antecedently to thought or choice of our own. We have created a new atmosphere, which we breathe into ourselves and by breathing which our composition is modified unawares, according to the ingredients which that atmosphere contains. I do not say that we are the creatures of what

---

treats (chap. iii. p. 41) the question, "Why does not religion reach the masses?" His conclusion is stated thus: "The weak point is clearly the loss of spiritual motive, and increased strength of natural motives as springs of action and thought."

surrounds us, for we have power to reflect upon and to control it. Yet, reflection and control are exercised but little, in comparison with the need for them; and, in the absence of such exercise, it is the surrounding atmosphere, it is the ordinary standard, accepted, and to a great extent necessarily accepted, without examination, that both supplies the stock wherewith we individually begin the great adventure of the world, and that guides our life, except in the rare cases where depravity on one side, or Christian heroism on the other, causes us to adopt a separate standard for ourselves. Where both range only within the zone marked out by fashionable opinion, it is sadly easy to point out men of high virtue with little creed, and men of low virtue with much creed, in the discipline and conduct of their personal lives respectively. And, in the region of opinion, it often seems as if liberty and justice among men fared quite as well with the heterodox, as with the orthodox.

A large part of these grave and even terrible anomalies is no doubt due to the fact, that to each of us personally our creed has come, not with the throes of struggle, sacrifice, and strong conviction, but rather, like most of what we hold—an easy tenure!—by descent, through others, not from ourselves; as matter of course, not of choice and effort; so that it sits upon us like an outward badge, rather than pervades us as a principle and a power.

But, on the other hand, how true it will be found that the sovereign tradition which has filled the air is the Christian tradition. This it is, which has made possible what without it would have been wholly beyond reach. This it is, which carries noiselessly into many minds and characters those opinions on behalf of virtue, of self-denial, and of philanthropy, together with the power of acting upon them, which are often found so honorably to distinguish creedless men. Just as many, who do not reject Christianity, know not why or how they came to hold it, so many, who have abjured Christianity, know not that, in the best of their thought, their nature, and their practice, they are appropriating its fruits. What is the modern word altruism? As to its meaning, it is simply the second great commandment of the Christian law, which was "like unto the first." As to its form, it is merely a disguise which has been put upon a borrowed idea, so that it often fails to be traced to its true original. And this not by a conscious, but, if the phrase may be pardoned, by an unconscious fraud. We find ourselves in possession of the code of Christian ethics, which has gradually pervaded life, institutions, manners, and has become so blended with our ordinary life that the memory of its divine origin has faded away, as though it were like the title-deed of some inheritance which we hold by unquestioned use. If we wish to know what the Christian tradition has done for us, we must examine the moral standard of nations who have differed from us mainly in not having it. For example, we must look to the Greeks of the fifth century before Christ, or the Romans at and after the period of the Advent, whose moral degradation was not less conspicuous than the intellectual splendor of the one, or the constructive political genius of the other.

My twofold proposition is that we have before us an increased power of things seen, and that this increased power implies a diminishing hold upon us of things unseen. The question is no new one. Throughout the history of mankind, the invisible, and the future which is part of the invisible, have been in standing competition with what may be termed the things of this world.

> "Two magnets, heaven and earth, allure to bliss;
> The larger loadstone that, the nearer this;
> The weak attraction of the greater fails,
> We nod awhile, but neighborhood prevails." *

There has never been a time in human

* Dryden, "Hind and Panther," part iii.

history to compare with the last half century in two vital respects; the multiplication of wealth, and the multiplication of the enjoyments which wealth procures; two things separate, yet concurrent, and morally allied. To take a familiar example: men (and the commodities they depend on) now travel at (say) one-fourth of the former cost, just when they have also an enlargement of their means to bear the cost of travelling. True, this pervading change has gone, to an immense extent, towards the cure of actual want, and towards extending the sphere of that sufficiency, that modest and humble comfort, which do not at all come within the scope of the present argument. But it has also extended largely to the spheres of leisure and of comparative affluence; and in those spheres it is generally true that the apparatus of enjoyment has been immensely developed in small things and great, that wants and appetites have grown along with it, and that if "the world was too much with us" when Wordsworth wrote his noble sonnet, it is more with us now than it was then. Obviously, almost mathematically, the increased powers of worldly attraction disturb the balance of our condition, unless and until they are compensated by increased powers of unworldly attraction and elevation. Whence are such compensating powers

to be had? I am afraid we can hardly say
that, in the spheres now under view, there
has been such a growth in unworldly
motives and ideas, as to countervail the
augmented strength of worldly attachment.
And I apprehend that, if the unseen world
and the ideas belonging to it operate upon
us with a proportionately diminished force,
it follows, almost as a matter of course, that
creeds, which belong to that circle of unseen
associations, will be more dimly and therefore more feebly appreciated. Materialism
as a formulated system is probably not upon
the increase. Those who think, as I am
compelled to think, about the intellectual
calibre and capabilities of such a system,
will hardly include such a growth among
the objects of their apprehension. But the
power of a silent, unavowed, unconscious
materialism is a very different matter. I
think Professor Max Müller has said that
without language there cannot be thought.
And this I suppose is true of all organized
and conscious thought. But there are in
human nature a multitude of undeveloped
(so to speak) embryonic forces, of impressions received from without, and finding a
congenial soil within, which never ripen to
maturity, or make their way into articulate
speech, or obtain a defined place in our
consciousness.

My belief is that at this moment these unspoken and untested movements, not so much of mind, as of appetite, or, to use a milder word, propensity, pressing upon mind, these not thoughts, but rudiments of thought, are at work among us, and within us ; and that, were they translated or expanded into words, their sense would be no more nor less than the old vulgar sense of those, who in every age have held that after all this world is the only world we securely know ; and that the only labor that is worth laboring, the only care worth caring, the only joy worth enjoying, are the labor, the care, the joy that begin and end with it. What can be more natural (in the lower sense of nature) than that among those on whom this world really smiles, together with the increasing gravitation towards a terrestrial centre, too often a creeping palsy should silently come over the inward life ? And how easy it is to understand that, when such a palsy has set in, a new and less ungenial color is imparted to whatever undermines the written Word, or the great Christian tradition, or in whatever other way repels, or blinds and deadens, the sense of the presence of God, and silences the reproaches of the voice within. So that it is not either real or pretended science, nor is it even the errors and excesses of believers, illegitimately charged upon belief, that form the root of the mischief. It is the increased force within us of all which is sensuous and worldly that furnishes every sceptical argument, good, bad, or indifferent, with an unseen ally, and that recruits many and many a disciple of the negative teaching. He indeed dreams that by the free admission of doubt he is paying homage to truth, when in reality he is only pampering the inferior life; for he allows fresh coadjutors, with unexamined credentials, to enter and to reinforce its already overweening power. Ideas in themselves weak are backed by propension, which is ever strong. A latent conspiracy is established, and two knights ride forth together to the war, one of them fairly exhibiting his countenance, but the other with his vizor down.

And the chain of cause and consequence is something like this. The Christian Creed generates a Christian tradition of idea and conduct. Of this tradition men do not disown the precepts; they only deny the parentage. And then there appears some great thinker, some really venerable man, who has learned to cherish piety, while he discards dogma. The next order of operators in the field carry the work a stage further, and cherish morality, while they discard piety. And the anti-moral, anti-spiritual force, that is strong even if it be hidden in us all, using what is substantive in the work as a cover for what is destructive, looks on with complacency, and swells the chorus of applause. The sceptical argument is in reality little more than a graft, set into, and deriving its life and energy mainly from, a tree stronger and more enduring than itself.

In thus stating my conviction that it is the great world-power within us and around us, which at the present time gives to scepticism the chief part of its breadth and its impetus, it will be seen that my remarks have little application to the officers or the soldiers of the army; to those who really, and it may be laboriously, think out subjects admitted to be arduous for themselves. They apply more to the camp-followers, who largely outnumber both, and whose voices are not less good than others to swell an acclamation, as Falstaff's recruits were not less good than others to fill a pit. The opinions of a man are due partly to himself, partly to his environment; in the thinking man mainly to himself, though even he may be affected by latent influences never consciously present to his thoughts; mainly, sometimes wholly, to environment in those who do not think; and environment, I need hardly say, includes the idols and the fancies, the shadows and the phantoms, of the passing day.

I must, however, in drawing these observations to a close, for a moment change my tone. In their nature apologetic, they themselves require an apology; and an apology, too, which is also in the nature of protest. They are intended to meet, so far as they go, a state of things peculiar and perhaps without example, in which multitudes of men call into question the foundations of our religion and the prerogatives of our sacred books, without any reference to either their capacity or their opportunities for so grave an undertaking. In other matters, qualification must be known or shown; in religion, it is taken for granted.

We have to bring equally into view, on the one side and on the other, two great propositions. On the one hand, the Christian religion stands on the foundation of free and intelligent assent. On the other hand every man, whatever be his position, founds, and reasonably, nay, necessarily founds, the actions and experiences of his life principally upon trust. Upon trust, no doubt, which is both intelligent and free; but still upon *trust*. Upon trust, sometimes in particular individuals, sometimes upon traditions which are, in a narrower or wider sphere, the traditions of his race. Every one acting a responsible part in the world, be it great or small, and be it acted with or without consciousness of its character, is continually working for others as well as for himself; is establishing and verifying on behalf of others, and in lieu of others, intellectual conclusions or material facts, which are needful for human life, but which the conditions of human life do not permit men in each case to establish and verify for themselves. Still, to establish and verify for ourselves is best. Independent knowledge is to be preferred where, and as, it can be had. The limiting law is found in capacity and in opportunity. Where we cannot, and this is often, let us refuse to seek refuge in the falsehood of a pretended or supposed examination.

But it seems to be beyond doubt that, more perhaps in these days than of old, numbers both of women and of men question the religion delivered to them from of old without, or in excess of, both capacity and opportunity. The turn and training of the mind, the nature of callings and pursuits, make it for some of us reasonable and necessary to put the great historic revelation on its trial as to its evidences of fact and doctrine, and its relation to the character and condition of man. This searching process is in itself thoroughly normal; and its application to the subject-matter, and the commonly affirmative results of such application, through so many ages and in minds so many and so great, have continually added force to the authority with which the Gospel lays claim to our assent and our obedience.

As to the mass of mankind, however, reason teaches that the presumption is for each man in favor of that which he has received, until he has found solid cause to question it. This is the rule taught by common sense, and established in common life. It is doubt, and not belief, of the things received, which ought in all cases to be put upon its defence, and to show its credentials: credentials, not necessarily in terms of demonstration, but of rational likelihood. But untested doubt, which often makes a lodgment in our minds, is a tenant without a title, a dangerous and in the main an unlawful guest. It assumes unawares, and in default of examination, the attitude of demonstrated negation. It paralyzes action; it casts into the shade the sense of duty, and of the Divine presence encompassing us in all our ways; and it reduces the pulse of our moral health. Doubt may emancipate us. Or it may enslave us. But it must be either a friend or an enemy: it cannot be a neutral. And those doubts, which cannot be tested, ought not to be entertained as having a title to affect conduct or belief. And such inquiries as, from being inadequate, are illusory, are but fresh forms of temptation from the path of duty. Inquiry should be undertaken as a solemn duty, when it can be made the subject of effective prosecution. But if we have not the means of effective prosecution, the so-called inquiry is a pretence and an imposture; and, under its name, we become the mere victims of assumptions due to prejudice, to fashion, to propensity, to appetite, to the insidious pressure of the world-power, to temptation in every one of its Protean shapes. The universal vocation of man is for each to regulate his own proper conduct in his own proper sphere. A noble task for all, but even this an arduous task; a task so arduous, that none can perform it in perfection. Duty does not require us to arrive at conclusions on

"Fixed fate, free-will, foreknowledge absolute,"

much less on the yet deeper and darker speculations which lie beyond, and which, so far as they are formidable, all run up into one single, one perhaps impenetrable problem, the presence and action of evil in the world. The Christian faith and the Holy Scriptures arm us with the means of neutralizing and repelling the assaults of evil in and from ourselves. That is a practical answer. Mist may rest upon the surrounding landscape, but our own path is visible from hour to hour, from day to day.

> "I do not ask to see
> The distant scene; one step enough for me."

Speculation, which is purposeless, becomes irreverent; and irreverent speculation on the doings and designs of God, by those who believe in Him, is itself a sin. To leave the duty of governing conduct, to which every one of us is called, for other functions to which we are not called, unless the power of following them reasonably guarantees our vocation for the work, is morally to pass from food to famine. It is as if one who possesses a piece or two of crockery full of cracks, should announce that he desires to give a sumptuous banquet to the neighborhood.

But besides acknowledging that the proper pre-conditions of legitimate inquiry are adequate capacity and adequate opportunity, and deploring the course of those who treat naked and unreasoned doubt as casting a burden of proof upon belief, we must bear in mind that religious inquiry, though it may raise conflicting issues, is not like a suit between parties who meet upon equal terms, or the conflict of Emperors warring for a territory in dispute. Our Saviour astonished the people because, instead of being lost in the mazes of arbitrary and vicious excrescences, that darkened the face of religion, He taught them "with authority, and not as the scribes." Taught them with authority, that is to say, with the title to command, and with the force of command. If God has given us a revelation of His will, whether in the laws of our nature, or in a kingdom of grace, that revelation not only illuminates, but binds. Like the credentials of an earthly ambassador, it is just and necessary that the credentials of that revelation should be tested. But if it be found genuine, if we have proofs of its being genuine equal to those of which, in the ordinary concerns of life, reason acknowledges the obligatory character, then we find ourselves to be not independent beings engaged in an optional inquiry, but the servants of a Master, the pupils of a Teacher, the children of a Father, and each of us already bound with the bonds which those relations imply. Then head and knee must bow before the Eternal, and the Divine will must be embraced and followed by man with all his heart, with all his mind, with all his soul, and with all his strength.

I have yet one more closing word. I have desired to make this humble offering at the shrine of Christian belief in general, and have sought wholly to avoid the questions which concern this or that particular form of it. For there is a common cause, which warrants and requires common efforts. Far be from me the intention hereby to undervalue particular beliefs. I have not intentionally said a word to disparage any of them. It will in my view be an evil day, and a day of calamity, when men are tempted, even by the vision of a holy object, to abate, in any region or in the smallest fraction, the authority of conscience, or to forget that the supreme title and the supreme efficacy of truth lie in its integrity.

Note on the Gadarene Miracle.

[The miracle of the possessed Gadarene, or Gergesene, raises in so pointed a form the question of demoniacal possession generally, that it has supplied the central point in the discussion of the case, and that other points, less salient on the surface, have received a smaller share of attention than they deserve.

The question may of course fairly be put, whether the movement of the devils by permission into the swine involved an injustice to an innocent owner, which would not be at all in harmony with the usually beneficent character of our Lord's ministry, and especially of His miracles.

Both Bishop Wordsworth * in his Commentary and Archbishop Trench refer to Josephus. The Bishop says, "Gadara is mentioned by Josephus as a Greek city, and hence the swine." I am, however, under the impression that both these excellent authors may have insufficiently examined the effect of the passages in Josephus, which relate to the subject. These, so far as I know, are three in number, and are found in the "Antiq. Jud.," xvii. 13, 4, and the "De Bello Jud.," iii. 7, 1, and iv. 7, 3. In the first-named of these Josephus undoubtedly says that Gadara was, like Gaza and Hippos, a Greek city, *Hellenis polis;* but he explains his meaning by adding, that these cities had been taken by the Roman authority out of the Diocese of Jerusalem, and added to that of Syria. The sense seems to be not that these cities were inhabited by a Greek population, but that they had politically been taken out of Judæa and added to Syria, which I presume

* *In loc.*, and Trench on the Miracles, p. 185.

was classified as simply Hellenic, a portion of the great Greek Empire erected by Alexander. As to the population of Gadara, the passage " De Bello Jud.," iii. 7, 1, appears absolutely to prove that it was a Jewish and not a Greek population; while Josephus also specifies, in " De Bello Jud.," iv. 7, 3, that many of the inhabitants were wealthy. For he mentions, in iii. 7, 1, that when Vespasian took the city he caused all the adult males to be put to death, and that he did this partly on account of a particular misdeed, but partly (*misei tou ethnous*) out of hatred towards the nation or race, evidently the Jewish nation, not possibly the Greek. The testimony of Josephus, therefore, does nothing to cast a doubt upon the natural, and in the absence of counter-evidence necessary, supposition that our Lord in this case had to deal with Hebrews, the ordinary subjects of His ministry, bound to the law of Moses, and on this occasion, as it would seem, justly punished for infringing it.

Hudson, in his commentary on Josephus, "Antiq. Jud.," xvii. 13, 4, gives a strong opinion, with his reasons, that Gadara is a wrong reading, and that we ought to read Gerasa. If he is right, the presumption founded on the phrase *Hellenis polis* at once disappears.]

HENRY ALTEMUS' PUBLICATIONS.

PHILADELPHIA, PA.

THE RISE OF THE DUTCH REPUBLIC (a History). By John Lothrop Motley. A new and handsome library edition of a Grand Historical Work. Embellished with over 50 full-page half-tone Engravings. Complete in two volumes—over 1,600 pages. Crown 8vo. Cloth, per set, $2.00. Half Morocco, gilt top, per set, $3.25.

QUO VADIS. A tale of the time of Nero, by Henryk Sienkiewicz. Complete and unabridged. Translated by Dr. S. A. Binton, author of "Ancient Egypt," etc., and S. Malevsky, with illustrations by M. DeLipman. Crown 8vo. Cloth, ornamental, 515 pages, $1.25.

WITH FIRE AND SWORD. By the author of "Quo Vadis." A tale of the past. Crown 8vo. 825 pages. $1.00.

PAN MICHAEL. By the author of "Quo Vadis." A historical tale. Crown 8vo. 530 pages. $1.00.

JULIAN, THE APOSTATE. By S. Mereshkovski. "A brilliant and effective picture of one of the most interesting characters in history, who had been shudderingly styled anti-Christ by the followers of the new faith. In descriptive beauty the work is fully equal to "Quo Vadis." Cloth 12mo. 450 pages. $1.00.

MANUAL OF MYTHOLOGY. For the use of Schools, Art Students, and General Readers, by Alexander S. Murray, Department of Greek and Roman Antiquities, British Museum. With Notes, Revisions, and Additions by William H. Klapp, Headmaster of the Protestant Episcopal Academy, Philadelphia. With 200 illustrations and an exhaustive Index. Large 12mo, 40 pages, $1.25.

THE AGE OF FABLE; OR, BEAUTIES OF MYTHOLOGY. By Thomas Bulfinch, with Notes, Revisions and Additions by William H. Klapp, Headmaster of the Protestant Episcopal Academy, Philadelphia. With 200 illustrations and an exhaustive Index. Large 12mo, 450 pages, $1.25.

This work has always been regarded as classical authority.

HENRY ALTEMUS' PUBLICATIONS.

TAINE'S ENGLISH LITERATURE, translated from the French by Henry Van Laun, illustrated with 20 fine photogravure portraits. Best English library edition, four volumes, cloth, full gilt, octavo, per set, $10.00. Half calf, per set, $12.50. Cheaper edition, with frontispiece illustrations only, cloth, paper titles, per set, $7.50.

STEPHEN. A SOLDIER OF THE CROSS, by Florence Morse Kingsley, author of "Titus, a Comrade of the Cross." "Since 'Ben-Hur' no story has so vividly portrayed the times of Christ."—"The Bookseller." Cloth, 12mo, 369 pages, $1.00.

THE CROSS TRIUMPHANT, by Florence Morse Kingsley, author of "Paul and Stephen." The story of "a child of the law," who witnesses, amid the scenes of the recent life and death of Jesus, the deepening conflict between the Law and the Cross. Nazarite, priest and warrior, influenced by three women of widely-varying character, he beholds at last in the terrible hour of Jerusalem's downfall "The Cross Triumphant." Cloth, 12mo, 364 pages, $1.00.

PAUL. A HERALD OF THE CROSS, by Florence Morse Kingsley. "A vivid and picturesque narrative of the life and times of the great Apostle." Cloth, 12mo, 450 pages, $1.00.

AMERICAN POLITICS (non-Partisan), by Hon. Thomas V. Cooper. A history of all the Political Parties, with their views and records on all important questions. All political platforms from the beginning. Great Speeches on Great Issues. Parliamentary practice and tabulated history of chronological events. A library without this work is deficient. 8vo, 750 pages. Cloth, $3.00. Full sheep, Library style, $4.00.

THE PILGRIM'S PROGRESS, as John Bunyan wrote it. A fac-simile reproduction of the first edition, published in 1678. Antique cloth, 12mo, $1.25.

THE FAIREST OF THE FAIR, by Hildegarde Hawthorne. "The grand-daughter of Nathaniel Hawthorne possesses a full share of his wonderful genius." Cloth, 16mo, $1.25.

HENRY ALTEMUS' PUBLICATIONS.

AROUND THE WORLD IN EIGHTY MINUTES. Contains over 100 photographs of the most famous places and edifices, with descriptive text. Cloth, 50 cents.

SHAKSPEARE'S COMPLETE WORKS, with a biographical sketch by Mary Cowden Clark, embellished with 64 Boydell, and numerous other illustrations, four volumes, over 2,000 pages. Half Morocco, 12mo, boxed, per set, $3.00.

THE CARE OF CHILDREN, by Elisabeth R. Scovil. "An excellent book of the most vital interest." Cloth, 12mo, $1.00.

PREPARATION FOR MOTHERHOOD, by Elisabeth R. Scovil. Cloth, 12mo, 320 pages, $1.00.

BABY'S REQUIREMENTS, by Elisabeth R. Scovil. Limp binding, leatherette, 25 cents.

NAMES FOR CHILDREN, by Elisabeth Robinson Scovil, author of "The Care of Children," "Preparation for Motherhood," etc. In family life there is no question of greater weight or importance than naming the baby. The author gives much good advice and many suggestions on the subject. Cloth, 12mo, 40 cents.

TRIF AND TRIXY, by John Habberton, author of "Helen's Babies." The story is replete with vivid and spirited scenes, and is comparatively the happiest and most delightful work Mr. Habberton has yet written. Cloth, 12mo, 50 cents.

SHE WHO WILL NOT WHEN SHE MAY, by Eleanor G. Walton. Half-tone illustrations by C. P. M. Rumford. "An exquisite prose idyl." Cloth, gilt top, deck'e edges, $1.00.

A SON OF THE CAROLINAS, by C. E. Satterthwaite. A pure romance introducing a lifelike portrayal of life on the coast islands of the Palmetto State. Cloth, 12mo, 280 pages, 50 cents.

THE DAY BREAKETH, by Fannie Alricks Shugert. A tale of Rome and Jerusalem in the time of Christ. Cloth, 12mo, 280 pages, 50 cents.

WHAT WOMEN SHOULD KNOW. A woman's book about women. By Mrs. E. B. Duffy. Cloth, 320 pages, 75 cents.

HENRY ALTEMUS' PUBLICATIONS.

THE DORE BIBLE GALLERY. A complete panorama of Bible History, containing 100 full-page engravings by Gustave Dore.

MILTON'S PARADISE LOST, with 50 full-page engravings by Gustave Dore.

DANTE'S INFERNO, with 75 full-page engravings by Gustave Dore.

DANTE'S PURGATORY AND PARADISE, with 60 full-page engravings by Gustave Dore.

TENNYSON'S IDYLLS OF THE KING, with 37 full-page engravings by Gustave Dore.

THE RIME OF THE ANCIENT MARINER, by Samuel Taylor Coleridge, with 46 full-page engravings by Gustave Dore.

Cloth, ornamental, large quarto (9x12 inches,), each $2.00.

BUNYAN'S PILGRIM'S PROGRESS, with 100 engravings by Frederick Barnard and others. Cloth, small quarto (9x10 inches), $1.00.

DICKENS' CHILD'S HISTORY OF ENGLAND, with 75 fine engravings by famous artists. Cloth, small quarto, boxed (9x10 inches), $1.00.

BIBLE PICTURES AND STORIES. 100 full-page engravings. Cloth, small quarto (7x9 inches), $1.00.

MY ODD LITTLE FOLK, some rhymes and verses about them, by Malcolm Douglass. Numerous original engravings. Cloth, small quarto (7x9 inches), $1.00.

PAUL AND VIRGINIA, by Bernardin de St. Pierre, with 125 engravings by Maurice Leloir. Cloth, small quarto (9x10), $1.00.

LIFE AND ADVENTURES OF ROBINSON CRUSOE. with 120 original engravings by Walter Paget. Cloth, octavo (7½x9¾), $1.50.

ALTEMUS' ILLUSTRATED LIBRARY OF STANDARD AUTHORS.

Cloth, 12mo. Size 5½x7¼ Inches. Each $1.00.

TALES FROM SHAKSPEARE, by Charles and Mary Lamb, with 155 illustrations by famous artists.

HENRY ALTEMUS' PUBLICATIONS.

PAUL AND VIRGINIA, by Bernardin de St. Pierre, with 125 engravings by Maurice Leloir.

ALICE'S ADVENTURES IN WONDERLAND, AND THROUGH THE LOOKING-GLASS AND WHAT ALICE FOUND THERE, by Lewis Carroll. Complete in one volume with 92 engravings by John Tenniel.

LUCILE, by Owen Meredith, with numerous illustrations by George Du Maurier, author of "Trilby."

BLACK BEAUTY, by Anna Sewell, with nearly 50 original engravings.

SCARLET LETTER, by Nathaniel Hawthorne, with numerous original full-page and text illustrations.

THE HOUSE OF THE SEVEN GABLES, by Nathaniel Hawthorne, with numerous original full-page and text illustrations.

BATTLES OF THE WAR FOR INDEPENDENCE, by Prescott Holmes, with 70 illustrations.

BATTLES OF THE WAR FOR THE UNION, by Prescott Holmes with 80 illustrations.

THE SONG OF HIAWATHA, by Henry W. Longfellow, with 100 illustrations.

ALTEMUS' YOUNG PEOPLES' LIBRARY.
Price, 50 cents each.

ROBINSON CRUSOE: (Chiefly in words of one syllable). His life and strange, surprising adventures, with 70 beautiful illustrations by Walter Paget.

ALICE'S ADVENTURES IN WONDERLAND. with 42 illustrations by John Tenniel. "The most delightful of children's stories. Elegant and delicious nonsense."—"Saturday Review."

THROUGH THE LOOKING-GLASS AND WHAT ALICE FOUND THERE: a companion to "Alice in Wonderland," with 50 illustrations by John Tenniel.

BUNYAN'S PILGRIM'S PROGRESS, with 50 full-page and text illustrations.

HENRY ALTEMUS' PUBLICATIONS.

Altemus' Young Peoples' Library—Continued.

A CHILD'S STORY OF THE BIBLE, with 72 full-page illustrations.

A CHILD'S LIFE OF CHRIST, with 49 illustrations. God has implanted in the infant heart a desire to hear of Jesus, and children are early attracted and sweetly riveted by the wonderful Story of the Master from the Manger to the Throne.

SWISS FAMILY ROBINSON, with 50 illustrations. The father of the family tells the tale of the vicissitudes through which he and his wife and children pass, the wonderful discoveries made and dangers encountered. The book is full of interest and instruction.

CHRISTOPHER COLUMBUS AND THE DISCOVERY OF AMERICA, with 70 illustrations. Every American boy and girl should be acquainted with the story of the life of the great discoverer, with its struggles, adventures, and trials.

THE STORY OF EXPLORATION AND DISCOVERY IN AFRICA, with 80 illustrations. Records the experiences of adventures and discoveries in developing the "Dark Continent," from the early days of Bruce and Mungo Park down to Livingstone and Stanley, and the heroes of our own times. No present can be more acceptable than such a volume as this, where courage, intrepidity, resource, and devotion are so admirably mingled.

THE FABLES OF ÆSOP. Compiled from the best accepted sources. With 62 illustrations. The fables of Æsop are among the very earliest compositions of this kind, and probably have never been surpassed for point and brevity.

GULLIVER'S TRAVELS. Adapted for young readers, with 50 illustrations.

MOTHER GOOSE'S RHYMES, JINGLES AND FAIRY TALES, with 234 illustrations.

HENRY ALTEMUS' PUBLICATIONS.

Altemus' Young People's' Library—Continued.

LIVES OF THE PRESIDENTS OF THE UNITED STATES, by Prescott Holmes. With portraits of the Presidents and also of the unsuccessful candidates for the office; as well as the ablest of the Cabinet officers. It is just the book for intelligent boys, and it will help to make them intelligent and patriotic citizens.

THE STORY OF ADVENTURE IN THE FROZEN SEAS, with 70 illustrations. By Prescott Holmes. We have here brought together the records of the attempts to reach the North Pole. The book shows how much can be accomplished by steady perseverance and indomitable pluck.

ILLUSTRATED NATURAL HISTORY, by the Rev. J. G. Wood, with 80 illustrations. This author has done more to popularize the study of natural history than any other writer. The illustrations are striking and life-like.

A CHILD'S HISTORY OF ENGLAND, by Charles Dickens, with 50 illustrations. Tired of listening to his children memorize the twaddle of old-fashioned English history, the author covered the ground in his own peculiar and happy style for his own children's use. When the work was published its success was instantaneous.

BLACK BEAUTY: THE AUTOBIOGRAPHY OF A HORSE, by Anna Sewell, with 50 illustrations. A work sure to educate boys and girls to treat with kindness all members of the animal kingdom. Recognized as the greatest story of animal life extant.

THE ARABIAN NIGHTS ENTERTAINMENTS, with 130 illustrations. Contains the most favorably known of the stories.

GRIMM'S FAIRY TALES. With 55 illustrations.
The Tales are a wonderful collection, as interesting, from a literary point of view, as they are delightful as stories.

FLOWER FABLES. By Louisa May Alcott. With numerous illustrations, full-page and text.
A series of very interesting fairy tales by the most charming of American story-tellers.

HENRY ALTEMUS' PUBLICATIONS.

Altemus' Young Peoples' Library—Continued.

ANDERSEN'S FAIRY TALES. By Hans Christian Andersen. With 77 illustrations.

    The spirit of high moral teaching, and the delicacy of sentiment, feeling, and expression that pervade these tales make these wonderful creations not only attractive to the young, but equally acceptable to those of mature years, who are able to understand their real significance and apprecciate the depth of their meaning.

GRANDFATHER'S CHAIR; A HISTORY FOR YOUTH. By Nathaniel Hawthorne. With 60 illustrations.

    The story of America from the landing of the Puritans to the acknowledgment without reserve of the Independence of the United States, told with all the elegance, simplicity, grace, clearness and force for which Hawthorne is conspicuously noted.

AUNT MARTHA'S CORNER CUPBOARD, by Mary and Elizabeth Kirby, with 60 illustrations. Stories about Tea, Coffee, Sugar, Rice and Chinaware, and other accessories of the well-kept Cupboard. A book full of interest for all the girls and many of the boys.

BATTLES OF THE WAR FOR INDEPENDENCE, by Prescott Holmes, with 70 illustrations. A graphic and full history of the Rebellion of the American Colonies from the yoke and oppression of England, with the causes that led thereto, and including an account of the second war with Great Britain, and the War with Mexico.

BATTLES OF THE WAR FOR THE UNION, by Prescott Holmes, with 80 illustrations. A correct and impartial account of the greatest civil war in the annals of history. Both of these histories of American wars are a necessary part of the education of all intelligent American boys and girls.

HENRY ALTEMUS' PUBLICATIONS.

ALTEMUS' KIPLING SERIES.

Embracing the best known tales and stories of this popular writer. Presented in attractive handy volume size, and adapted for leisure moment reading. Large type, superior paper and attractive binding. Cloth, 35 cents.

1. THE DRUMS OF THE FORE AND AFT.
2. THE MAN WHO WAS.
3. WITHOUT BENEFIT OF CLERGY.
4. RECRUDESCENCE OF IMRAY.
5. ON GREENHOW HILL.
6. WEE WILLIE WINKIE.
7. THE MAN WHO WOULD BE KING.
8. MY OWN TRUE GHOST STORY.
9. THE COURTING OF DINAH SHADD.
10. THE INCARNATION OF KRISHNA MULVANEY.
11. HIS MAJESTY THE KING.
12. WITH THE MAIN GUARD.
13. THE THREE MUSKETEERS.
14. LISPETH.
15. CUPID'S ARROWS.
16. IN THE HOUSE OF SUDDHOO.
17. THE BRONCKHORST DIVORCE-CASE.
18. THE JUDGMENT OF DUNGARA.
19. GEMINI.
20. AT TWENTY-TWO.
21. ON THE CITY WALL.

ALTEMUS' ILLUSTRATED ONE SYLLABLE SERIES FOR YOUNG READEARS.

Embracing popular works arranged for the young folks in words of one syllable.

Printed from extra large clear type on fine enamelled paper and fully illustrated by famous artists. The handsomest line of books for young children before the public.

Fine English cloth; handsome, new, original designs, 50 cents.

1. ÆSOP'S FABLES. 62 illustrations.
2. A CHILD'S LIFE OF CHRIST. 49 illustrations.

HENRY ALTEMUS' PUBLICATIONS.

One Syllable Series—Continued.

3. A CHILD'S STORY OF THE BIBLE. 72 illustrations.
4. THE ADVENTURES OF ROBINSON CRUSOE. 70 illustrations.
5. BUNYAN'S PILGRIM'S PROGRESS. 46 illustrations.
6. SWISS FAMILY ROBINSON. 50 illustrations.
7. GULLIVER'S TRAVELS. 50 illustrations.

HENRY ALTEMUS' PUBLICATIONS.

ALTEMUS' NEW ILLUSTRATED VADEMECUM SERIES.

Masterpieces of English and American literature, handy volume size, large type editions. Each volume contains illuminated title pages, etched portrait of author or colored frontispiece and numerous engravings.

Full cloth, ivory finish, ornamental inlaid sides and back, boxed, 40 cents.

1. ABBE CONSTANTIN.—Ha'evy.
2. ADVENTURES OF A BROWNIE.—Mulock.
3. ALICE'S ADVENTURES IN WONDERLAND.—Carroll.
4. AMERICAN NOTES.—Kipling.
5. AUTOBIOGRAPHY OF BENJAMIN FRANKLIN.
6. AUTOCRAT OF THE BREAKFAST TABLE.—Holmes.
11. BAB BALLADS AND SAVOY SONGS.—Gilbert.
12. BACON'S ESSAYS.
13. BALZAC'S SHORTER STORIES.
14. BARRACK-ROOM BALLADS AND DITTIES.—Kipling.
15. BATTLE OF LIFE.—Dickens.
16. BIGLOW PAPERS.—Lowell.
17. BLACK BEAUTY.—Sewell.
18. BLITHEDALE ROMANCE, THE.—Hawthorne.
19. BRACEBRIDGE HALL.—Irving.
20. BRYANT'S POEMS.
26. CAMILLE.—Dumas, Jr.
27. CARMEN.—Merimee.

HENRY ALTEMUS' PUBLICATIONS.

Vademecum Series—Continued.

28. CHARLOTTE TEMPLE.—Rowson.
29. CHESTERFIELD'S LETTERS, SENTENCES AND MAXIMS.
30. CHILD'S GARDEN OF VERSES.—Stevenson.
31. CHILDE HAROLD'S PILGRIMAGE.—Byron.
32. CHIMES, THE.—Dickens.
33. CHRISTIE'S OLD ORGAN.—Walton.
34. CHRISTMAS CAROL, A.—Dickens.
35. CONFESSIONS OF AN OPIUM EATER.—De Quincey.
36. CRANFORD.—Gaskell.
37. CRICKET ON THE HEARTH.—Dickens.
38. CROWN OF WILD OLIVE, THE.—Ruskin.
43. DAY BREAKETH, THE.—Shugert.
44. DAYS WITH SIR ROGER DE COVERLY.—Addison.
45. DISCOURSES, EPICTETUS.
46. DOG OF FLANDERS, A.—Ouida.
47. DREAM LIFE.—Mitchell.
51. EMERSON'S ESSAYS, FIRST SERIES.
52. EMERSON'S ESSAYS, SECOND SERIES.
53. ENDYMION.—Keats.
54. ESSAYS OF ELIA.—Lamb.
55. ETHICS OF THE DUST.—Ruskin.
56. EVANGELINE.—Longfellow.
61. FAIRY LAND OF SCIENCE.—Buckley.
62. FANCHON.—Sand.
63. FOR DAILY BREAD.—Sienkiewicz.
67. GRAMMAR OF PALMISTRY.—St. Hill.
68. GREEK HEROES.—Kingsley.
69. GULLIVER'S TRAVEL'S.—Swift.
74. HANIA.—Sienkiewicz.
75. HAUNTED MAN, THE.—Dickens.
76. HEROES AND HERO WORSHIP.—Carlyle.
77. HIAWATHA, THE SONG OF.—Longfellow.
78. HOLME'S POEMS.
79. HOUSE OF THE SEVEN GABLES.—Hawthorne.
80. HOUSE OF THE WOLF.—Weyman.
81. HYPERION.—Longfellow.
87. IDLE THOUGHTS OF AN IDLE FELLOW.—Jerome.
88. IDYLLS OF THE KING.—Tennyson.
89. IMPREGNABLE ROCK OF HOLY SCRIPTURE.—Gladstone.

HENRY ALTEMUS' PUBLICATIONS.

Vademecum Series—Continued.

90. IN BLACK AND WHITE.—Kipling.
91. IN MEMORIAM.—Tennyson.
96. JESSICA'S FIRST PRAYER.—Stretton.
97. J. COLE.—Gellibrand.
101. KAVANAGH.—Longfellow.
102. KIDNAPPED.—Stevenson.
103. KNICKERBOCKER'S HISTORY OF NEW YORK.—Irving.
107. LA BELLE NIVERNAISE.—Daudet.
108. LADDIE AND MISS TOOSEY'S MISSION.
109. LADY OF THE LAKE.—Scott.
110. LALLA ROOKH.—Moore.
111. LAST ESSAYS OF ELIA.—Lamb.
112. LAYS OF ANCIENT ROME, THE.—Macaulay.
113. LET US FOLLOW HIM.—Sienkiewicz.
114. LIGHT OF ASIA.—Arnold.
115. LIGHT THAT FAILED, THE.—Kipling.
116. LITTLE LAME PRINCE.—Mulock.
117. LONGFELLOW'S POEMS, VOL. I.
118. LONGFELLOW'S POEMS, VOL. II.
119. LOWELL'S POEMS.
120. LUCILE.—Meredith.
126. MAGIC NUTS, THE.—Molesworth.
127. MANON LESCAUT.—Prevost.
128. MARMION.—Scott.
129. MASTER OF BALLANTRAE, THE.—Stevenson
130. MILTON'S POEMS.
131. MINE OWN PEOPLE.—Kipling.
132. MINISTER OF THE WORLD.—Mason.
133. MOSSES FROM AN OLD MANSE.—Hawthorne
134. MULVANEY STORIES.—Kipling.
140. NATURAL LAW IN THE SPIRITUAL WORLD.—Drummond.
141. NATURE, ADDRESSES, AND LECTURES.—Emerson.
145. OLD CHRISTMAS.—Irving.
146. OUTRE-MER.—Longfellow.
150. PARADISE LOST.—Milton.
151. PARADISE REGAINED.—Milton.
152. PAUL AND VIRGINIA.—Sainte Pierre.
153. PETER SCHLEMIHL.—Chamisso.
154. PHANTOM RICKSHAW.—Kipling.
155. PILGRIM'S PROGRESS, THE.—Bunyan.

HENRY ALTEMUS' PUBLICATIONS.

Vademecum Series—Continued.

156. PLAIN TALES FROM THE HILLS.—Kipling.
157. PLEASURES OF LIFE.—Lubbock.
158. PLUTARCH'S LIVES.
159. POE'S POEMS.
160. PRINCE OF THE HOUSE OF DAVID.—Ingraham.
161. PRINCESS AND MAUD.—Tennyson.
162. PRUE AND I.—Curtis.
169. QUEEN OF THE AIR.—Ruskin.
172. RAB AND HIS FRIENDS.—Brown.
173. REPRESENTATIVE MEN.—Emerson.
174. REVERIES OF A BACHELOR.—Mitchell.
175. RIP VAN WINKLE.—Irving.
176. ROMANCE OF A POOR YOUNG MAN.—Feuillet.
177. RUBAIYAT OF OMAR KHAYYAM.—
182. SAMANTHA AT SARATOGA.—Holley.
183. SARTOR RESARTUS.—Carlyle.
184. SCARLET LETTER, THE.—Hawthorne.
185. SCHOOL FOR SCANDAL.—Sheridan.
186. SENTIMENTAL JOURNEY, A.—Sterne.
187. SESAME AND LILIES.—Ruskin.
188. SHAKSPEARE'S HEROINES.—Jameson.
189. SHE STOOPS TO CONQUER.—Goldsmith.
190. SILAS MARNER.—Eliot.
191. SKETCH BOOK, THE.—Irving.
192. SNOW IMAGE, THE.—Hawthorne.
199. TALES FROM SHAKSPEARE.—Lamb.
200. TANGLEWOOD TALES.—Hawthorne.
201. TARTARIN OF TARASCON.—Daudet.
202. TARTARIN ON THE ALPS.—Daudet.
203. TEN NIGHTS IN A BAR-ROOM.—Arthur.
204. THINGS WILL TAKE A TURN.—Harraden.
205. THOUGHTS.—MARCUS AURELIUS.
206. THROUGH THE LOOKING GLASS.—Carroll.
207. TOM BROWN'S SCHOOL DAYS.—Hughes.
208. TREASURE ISLAND.—Stevenson.
209. TWICE TOLD TALES.—Hawthorne.
210. TWO YEARS BEFORE THE MAST.—Dana.
217. UNCLE TOM'S CABIN.—Stowe.
218. UNDINE.—Fouque.
222. VIC: THE AUTOBIOGRAPHY OF A FOX-TERRIER.—Marsh.

HENRY ALTEMUS' PUBLICATIONS.

Vademecum Series—Continued.

223. VICAR OF WAKEFIELD.—Goldsmith.
226. WALDEN.—Thoreau.
227. WATER BABIES.—Kingsley.
228. WEIRD TALES.—Poe.
229. WHAT IS ART?—Tolstoi.
230. WHITTIER'S POEMS, VOL. I.
231. WHITTIER'S POEMS, VOL. II.
232. WINDOW IN THRUMS.—Barrie.
233. WOMAN'S WORK IN THE HOME.—Farrar.
234. WONDER BOOK, A.—Hawthorne.
241. YELLOWPLUSH PAPERS, THE.—Thackeray.
244. ZOE.—By author of "Laddie," etc.

ALTEMUS' ILLUSTRATED DEVOTIONAL SERIES.

Full White Vellum, handsome new mosaic design in gold and colors, gold edges, Boxed, 50 cents.

1. ABIDE IN CHRIST.—Murray.
2. AT THE BEAUTIFUL GATE.
3. BEECHER'S ADDRESSES.
4. BEST THOUGHTS.—From Henry Drummond.
5. BIBLE BIRTHDAY BOOK.
6. BROOKS' ADDRESSES.
7. CHAMBER OF PEACE.
8. CHANGED CROSS, THE.
9. CHRISTIAN LIFE.—Oxenden.
10. CHRISTIAN LIVING.—Meyer.
11. CHRISTIAN'S SECRET OF A HAPPY LIFE.
12. CHRISTIE'S OLD ORGAN.—Walton.
13. COMING TO CHRIST.—Havergal.
14. DAILY FOOD FOR CHRISTIANS.
15. DAY BREAKETH, THE.—Shugert.
16. DAYS OF GRACE.—Murray.
17. DRUMMOND'S ADDRESSES.
18. EVENING THOUGHTS.—Havergal.
19. GOLD DUST.
20. HOLY IN CHRIST.—Murray.
21. IMITATION OF CHRIST, THE.—A'Kempis.
22. IMPREGNABLE ROCK OF HOLY SCRIPTURE.—Gladstone.

HENRY ALTEMUS' PUBLICATIONS.

Devotional Series—Continued.

23. JESSICA'S FIRST PRAYER.—Stretton.
24. JOHN PLOUGHMAN'S PICTURES.—Spurgeon.
25. JOHN PLOUGHMAN'S TALK.—Spurgeon.
26. KEPT FOR THE MASTER'S USE.—Havergal.
27. KEBLE'S CHRISTIAN YEAR.
28. LET US FOLLOW HIM.—Sienkiewicz.
29. LIKE CHRIST.—Murray.
30. LINE UPON LINE.
31. MANLINESS OF CHRIST, THE.—Hughes.
32. MESSAGE OF PEACE, THE.—Church.
33. MORNING THOUGHTS.—Havergal.
34. MY KING AND HIS SERVICE.—Havergal.
35. NATURAL LAW IN THE SPIRITUAL WORLD.—Drummond.
36. PALACE OF THE KING.
37. PATHWAY OF PROMISE.
38. PATHWAY OF SAFETY.—Oxenden.
39. PEEP OF DAY.
40. PILGRIM'S PROGRESS, THE.—Bunyan.
41. PRECEPT UPON PRECEPT.
42. PRINCE OF THE HOUSE OF DAVID—Ingraham.
43. SHADOW OF THE ROCK.
44. SHEPHERD PSALM.—Meyer.
45. STEPS INTO THE BLESSED LIFE.—Meyer.
46. STEPPING HEAVENWARD.—Prentiss.
47. THE THRONE OF GRACE.
48. UNTO THE DESIRED HAVEN.
49. UPLANDS OF GOD.
50. WITH CHRIST.—Murray.

ALTEMUS' EDITION SHAKSPEARE PLAYS.
HANDY VOLUME SIZE.

Limp cloth binding, gold top, illuminated title and frontispiece, 35 cents.

1. ALL'S WELL THAT ENDS WELL.
2. ANTONY AND CLEOPATRA.
3. A MIDSUMMER NIGHT'S DREAM.
4. AS YOU LIKE IT.
5. COMEDY OF ERRORS.
6. CORIOLANUS.
7. CYMBELINE.
8. HAMLET.
9. JULIUS CÆSAR.
10. KING HENRY IV. (Part I).
11. KING HENRY IV. (Part II).
12. KING HENRY V.
13. KING HENRY VI. (Part I).
14. KING HENRY VI. (Part II).
15. KING HENRY VI. (Part III).
16. KING HENRY VIII.
17. KING JOHN.
18. KING LEAR.
19. KING RICHARD II.
20. KING RICHARD III.
21. LOVE'S LABOUR'S LOST.
22. MACBETH.
23. MEASURE FOR MEASURE.
24. MUCH ADO ABOUT NOTHING.
25. OTHELLO.
26. PERICLES.
27. ROMEO AND JULIET.
28. THE MERCHANT OF VENICE.
29. THE MERRY WIVES OF WINDSOR.
30. THE TAMING OF THE SHREW.
31. THE TEMPEST.
32. THE TWO GENTLEMEN OF VERONA.
33. THE WINTER'S TALE.
34. TIMON OF ATHENS.
35. TITUS ANDRONICUS.
36. TROILUS AND CRESSIDA.
37. TWELFTH NIGHT.
38. VENUS AND ADONIS AND LUCRECE.
39. SONNETS, PASSIONATE PILGRIM, ETC.

www.ingramcontent.com/pod-product-compliance
Lightning Source LLC
Chambersburg PA
CBHW031847220426
43663CB00006B/529